LOOK, LISTEN, READ

Other Books by Claude Lévi-Strauss

The Savage Mind (1963)

Structural Anthropology, Volume I (1963)

Totemism (1963)

Elementary Structures of Kinship (1969)

The Raw and the Cooked,
Volume I in the Science of Mythology Series (1970)

From Honey to Ashes,
Volume II in the Science of Mythology Series (1973)

Tristes Tropiques (1974)

Structural Anthropology, Volume II (1976)

The Origin of Table Manners,
Volume III in the Science of Mythology Series (1979)

The Naked Man,
Volume IV in the Science of Mythology Series (1981)

The Way of the Masks (1982)

The View from Afar (1985)

Anthropology & Myth (1987)

The Jealous Potter (1988)

Conversations with Claude Lévi-Strauss (1991)

The Story of Lynx (1995)

LOOK, LISTEN, READ

CLAUDE LÉVI-STRAUSS

Translated by Brian C. J. Singer

BASIC
BOOKS

A Member of the Perseus Books Group

Originally published as *Regarder, Écouter, Lire,*
Copyright © 1993 by Librairie Plon.

Translation © 1997 by HarperCollins Publishers.

Published by Basic Books,
A Member of the Perseus Books Group.

Designed by Elliott Beard

Library of Congress Cataloging-in-Publication Data
Lévi-Strauss, Claude
  [Regarder, écouter, lire. English]
    Look, listen, read / by Claude Lévi-Strauss. — 1st ed.
      p. cm.
    ISBN 0-465-06880-4 (cloth) — ISBN 0-465-06881-2 (paper)
    1. Arts—Psychological aspects. 2. Artists—Psychology. I. Title.
NX165.L4513   1997
700'.1'9—dc21   96-51629
                                                                   CIP

98 99 00 01 ❖/RRD 10 9 8 7 6 5 4 3 2 1

Contents

Looking at Poussin   3

Listening to Rameau   39

Reading Diderot   63

Speech and Music   89

Sounds and Colors   127

Regarding Objects   157

Works Cited   187

Index   199

LOOK, LISTEN, READ

Looking at Poussin

I

Proust composed Vinteuil's sonata and its "little phrase" from his own impressions of pieces by Schubert, Wagner, Franck, Saint-Saëns, and Fauré. One sometimes wonders whether he was thinking of Manet, Monet, or even Patinir while describing the Elstir painting. The names of the writers who inspired his character Bergotte are equally uncertain.

Such syncretism, free from the constraints of time, goes together with a freedom in Proust's works that allows events or incidents belonging to different time periods to be evoked indiscriminately in the present. In one page, the narrator's words and thoughts seem to point to, variously, the ages of eight, twelve, or eighteen. Of his stay at Balbec with his grandmother, he says, "There [is] so little chronology in our life."

Regarding these matters, Jean-Louis Curtis has written a fine passage:

> In *Remembrance of Things Past*, time is neither lost nor found; the only time there is is without past or future, that is, the time specific to artistic creation. That is why the chronology in *Remembrance of Things Past* is so hazy, elusive and fleeting: time appears drawn out or cut short, or even circular—never linear; and of course, dates are never specified. . . . The reader wonders whether the children on the Champs-Elysées are still playing hoops or already puffing at their first clandestine cigarette.

Seen from this perspective, uncontrolled memory is not simply opposed to conscious memory (which allows one to recall the past without having to relive it). Uncontrolled memory breaks into the story line; it readjusts and restabilizes the composition, systematically altering the course and order of events. And in truth, Proust handles time's unfolding rather casually: "Some critics," he says, "now liked to regard the novel as a sort of procession of things upon the screen of a cinematograph. This comparison was absurd. Nothing is further from what we have really perceived than the vision that the cinematograph presents."

His reasons for taking such a stance are not only, perhaps not chiefly, philosophical or aesthetic. They are indissociable from his technique. *Remembrance of Things Past* consists of pieces written under various circumstances and during different periods. The author had to place them in the right order, which is to say, in the order corresponding to his own notion of truthfulness. Or at least in the beginning, for this order became harder and harder to sustain as the work progressed. On several occasions "odds and ends" had to be accommodated, with the ill-matched pieces becoming increasingly noticeable. Toward the end of *Time Regained,* Proust compared his work to that of a seamstress who was sewing a dress made from disparate pieces already cut to form, or who was patching a dress in tatters. In a similar way, his book is made from fragments that he had to piece together "in order to express a psychological truth, by grafting on to the movement of someone's shoulder a movement of the neck made by someone else." He had to conceive a single sonata, church, or young girl out of impressions culled from several sonatas, churches, or girls.

With such a cut-and-paste technique, the work proceeds from a double articulation. Though I am not using this term in its linguistic sense, it is not without relevance, for the units of the first articulation are already literary works that are then combined and organized into a literary work of a higher order. This type of composition is different from one that fuses various outlines and sketches into a single definitive version; here, the completed work resembles a mosaic where each piece retains its own face and character.

2

Similar phenomena can be found in painting. I believe Meyer Schapiro was the first to point out the patent discrepancies in scale among the characters in *La Grande Jatte*.* Is it not possible that Seurat first imagined his figures, or groups of figures, as independent units, which he then arranged relative to each other into a larger whole—probably after having experimented with several tries? Hence, to use one of Diderot's favorite words, the "magical" quality of *La Grande Jatte*, which shows a public place favored by strollers, strewn with characters or groups of characters seemingly heedless of each other's presence, frozen in their isolation. They are not unlike those "mute things" (in the words of Delacroix) that Poussin professed to work with: thus the uniquely mysterious atmosphere exuded by Seurat's painting.

A Sunday Afternoon on La Grande Jatte.

Diderot would have shunned such mystery:

> One may distinguish two kinds of composition, the picturesque and the expressive. Little do I care if the artist has exposed his figures to the most intriguing effects of light, as long as the whole does not speak to my soul; if the characters in the picture seem like fellows passing each other blindly in a public garden. . . .

It almost sounds like the exact anticipation, and a definitive condemnation, of the very spirit of Seurat's *Grande Jatte*.

One can find the same type of composition already in Hokusai, as can be seen in several pages from his *Hundred Views of Mount Fuji*. Just as Proust worked from scraps of paper, Hokusai used details, fragments of landscapes that he had probably sketched on the spot in his notebooks, and transferred to his compositions regardless of the differences in scale.

Yet more than any other painter, Poussin provides one of the best illustrations of such double articulation. Granted the differences, it still explains his "mineralized" figures, a bit like those in *La Grande Jatte* (his genius, said Philippe de Champaigne, "had a great capacity for solids"). One also sees why Diderot called his figures "naïve," "that is, being most perfectly and purely what they must be"; and why Delacroix talked of a primitivist attitude in his art, where "frankness of expression is never spoiled by any habit of execution"—a manner that makes of Poussin "an innovator of the rarest kind," true to his "independence from all convention."

When looking at Poussin, one cannot help but feel that he is reinventing painting, or at the very least, that he is stretching his hands beyond the century of his birth (the sixteenth) toward the great masters of the quattrocento, and first among them, Mantegna (during my first year at the *lycée*, at a time when my father

Giovanni Francesco Guercino
Et in Arcadia Ego
Rome, Galleria Corsini
(Photo Artephot/Fabbri)

Nicolas Poussin
Et in Arcadia Ego
(Les Bergers d'Arcadie, first version)
Chatsworth, Derbyshire, the Trustees of the Chatsworth Settlement

Nicolas Poussin
Et in Arcadia Ego
(Les Bergers d'Arcardie, second version)
Paris, Musée du Louvre
(Photo R.M.N.)

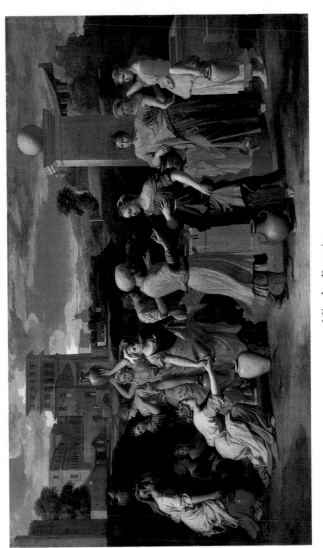

Nicolas Poussin
Eliezer et Rebecca
Paris, Musée du Louvre
(Photo R.M.N.)

often took me to the Louvre, I had to write an essay about my favorite painting; I chose his *Parnassus*).

Poussin perhaps had his sights set even farther, for his imagination sometimes displays that same ingenuousness, though magnified by the sublime touch of his genius, which, toward the end of the nineteenth century, Rimbaud sought in the gaudy paintings of fairground attractions. Thus, in *Vénus montrant ses armes à Énée,** on exhibit at the Rouen Museum, the goddess floating in the air at arm's length seems to have been designed and painted separately from the rest of the painting and then simply copied onto the canvas. The same again for the dryad in *Apollon amoureux de Daphné* [†] at the Louvre: she is, curiously enough, comfortably reclining among the foliage of too small an oak, as on a sofa bed. See also *Orion aveugle,* [‡] where Diane is resting her elbow on a cloud as though she were a matron posing before the mantelpiece in her sitting room.

Delacroix may well have had such matters in mind when he decried the "extreme dryness [of] Poussin's pictures . . . as if all the figures were without connection with one another; they seem cut out." Here is the spatial counterpart to what Proust does with time. In Delacroix's eyes, such dryness is a shortcoming, and he was certainly right to understand it in terms of what I am calling double articulation:

> Poussin never attempted [perfection]; he never even sought it out. His figures stand next to each other like statues. Could this be because—so the tradition goes—he always built small

---

Venus Presenting Arms to Aeneas.

[†] *Apollo and Daphne.*

[‡] *Blind Orion Searching for the Rising Sun.*

three-dimensional models of his prospective paintings in order
to get the right angles for the shadows?

And elsewhere he speaks of "little stage models lit up by the
studio light."

In 1721, Antoine Coypel also deplored in Poussin's figures
"the lack of a deportment more in keeping with nature, less dry
and stiff, freer from the forms imposed by his mannequins in their
wet drapings." Ingres, for his part, was more sensible when making the following note: "Make yourself a little peep-show cabinet,
like that which Poussin used: indispensable in judging effects."

(Incidentally, a contemporary commentator attributed to
Poussin the following reflections, which establish a parallel between articulated speech and painting, thus anticipating the linguistic theory of double articulation: "In his discourse upon
painting, quoth . . . as the twenty-four letters in the alphabet serve
to form our words and express our thoughts, so the lineaments of
the human body serve to express the diverse passions of the soul
and give outward form to what lies within the mind.")

It is well known that Poussin liked to work with wax. Early in
his career, he used it to copy antique statuary, or even to make bas
relief reproductions of fragments from the great masters' works. As
several witnesses recorded, before undertaking a new painting,
Poussin would shape little wax figures, stand them on a small board,
and pose them according to the way he imagined the scene. Then
he draped them in wet paper or light taffeta, molding the folds with
a thin pointed stick. With the whole set before him, he would begin to paint. The walls of the box had holes bored in them, allow-
ing him to light the scene from either the sides, the front, or the
back, and thus check the exact positions of the shadows. No doubt
he also experimented with various stagings of the figures, using the
scale model to perfect the composition of the scene on canvas.

Such a device was not unknown to his precursors. However, according to Anthony Blunt, it had become obsolete by Poussin's period because it demanded too much time. It is thus significant that Poussin took it up again and, as the sources testify, applied it meticulously. In no other painter is the systematic use of the three-dimensional model so perceptible; its presence is clearly visible behind the completed work. His figures seem not so much painted onto the canvas as sculpted into some improbable mass.

He had so completely assimilated this compositional technique that it almost became a way of thinking. This can be seen in his landscapes or urban scenes, which, arranged with great care, invite the beholder to venture along a number of potential itineraries. "There seem to be paths open before us in all the countries he depicts," says Félibien. In effect, with the contemplation of Poussin's paintings, one prolongs in time what has already been extended in space. The three dimensions granted to objects contrast with his frequently two-dimensional characters (arranged, some critics have said, as in bas relief). The third dimension conveys the dominance of the world over individuals. Poussin's age, interestingly enough, was shortly followed by the invention of three-dimensional maps, whose effect on the viewer is equally magical.

It seems to me that one of the reasons for Poussin's originality, and for the monumental quality that so impressed Delacroix, lies in the fact that his paintings proceed from a second articulation: the first articulation was already present in the model that stood as a work of art in its own right, only achieved with different, simpler means. At that first stage, art is already an imposing expression of a sort of *bricolage* Poussin excels in, and which perhaps lent him "the capacity for spreading out imposing and intricate compositions in small spaces," to quote Félibien.

Admittedly, nothing is more foreign to the bursts of inspiration that impelled romantic creation. Thus Delacroix's hesitations, which at times prompted him, despite his admiration for Poussin, to prefer Le Sueur:

> He has the art which is completely lacking in Poussin, of giving unity to everything he represents. A figure by him is in itself a perfect ensemble of lines and of effects, and the picture, the sum of all the figures united, is harmonized everywhere.

Delacroix's criticisms may be disconcerting, though they recall his fleeting preference for Cimarosa over Mozart in the realm of music. He deemed Cimarosa "more dramatic" and praised "that proportion, that breeding, that expression, that gaiety, that tenderness, and beyond all else . . . that incomparable elegance . . . not more of perfection, but perfection itself." He denied such perfection in Mozart, just as he denied it in Poussin.

From Delacroix's perspective, if Poussin paved the way for modern art (which seeks out "at the very source of things the effect on the imagination that is proper to the realm of painting"), he did so in a rather negative way, by breaking with convention. Did he really believe that Le Sueur went farther on this path than Poussin (in the passage quoted, he is associated with, rather than opposed to Poussin)? One cannot help thinking that, though Poussin and Le Sueur both "recall the naïveté of the primitives of Flanders and of Italy," Poussin nevertheless remained for Delacroix Le Sueur's "primitive" counterpart.

3

In an essay on Poussin's *Et in Arcadia ego*, Panofsky demonstrates three points:

1: The *Et in Arcadia* motto first appeared on a painting by Guercino dated circa 1621–1623, shortly before Poussin's arrival in Rome. The painting represents two shepherds meditating before a large skull set on a rock in the foreground.

2: When properly translated, the Latin formula does not mean "I too have lived in Arcadia"—the usual interpretation; rather, it means (as educated people knew well) "I too am here, I can be found even in Arcadia." It is Death itself speaking in the guise of the skull, to remind men of their inescapable fate, even in the sweetest clime.

3: Poussin first drew inspiration directly from Guercino, in a painting on the same theme probably dated circa 1629–1630; here the words are engraved onto a stone sarcophagus and cannot be interpreted differently. Though the skull on the tomb is quite small and barely visible, it (or else the tomb itself, as a symbol of death) is still speaking.

According to Panofsky, however, the second version of *Et in Arcadia ego* (at the Louvre), which was done five or six years later (circa 1638–1639 according to Thuillier), appears to suggest that Poussin altered the meaning of the motto, giving it the sense it would commonly bear by the end of the seventeenth century: "Poussin's Louvre picture no longer shows a dramatic encounter with Death but a contemplative absorption in the idea of mortality."

In my view, though, Panofsky overlooked an important fact: the first version is not merely an imitation of Guercino's painting, but marks a transitional stage between the latter and the Louvre picture. It bears witness to the evolution of Poussin's plastic imagination, without necessarily corresponding to the clear break of Panofsky's hypothesis.

One will note, for a start, the two differences between the first version and the work by Guercino. The skull has been moved back into the middle distance and is now so small as to seem insignificant; in the second version, it disappears altogether. Moreover, Poussin's early version shows a shepherdess in the background, where Guercino had none. In the Louvre picture, an imposing female figure stands in the foreground, and she is no longer lightly dressed like a shepherdess, but amply draped in the ancient manner, in contrast to the half-naked shepherds.

It is as if the large skull that stands in the foreground to the right in Guercino's painting has ceded its place to the woman who stands in the same position and takes on the same importance in Poussin's second version; and as if the first version—with the skull reduced to a recollection, and the discrete appearance of a female figure in the background—constituted an intermediate stage.

It would be tempting to interpret a third difference between the two versions in a similar manner. According to specialists, the old man sitting on the right in the foreground of the first version was placed there by Poussin as a symmetrical counterpart to a figure in what was to be a matching painting. Yet this old man, sitting in place of the skull in Guercino's picture, represents Alpheus, the river whose source lies in Arcadia. It was thought that this river crossed the sea to Sicily, to meet up with Arethusa, a nymph who had been changed into a fountain. As an intermediary version, could not the symbolic image of the river, or rather of the flow of its waters, be placed there to guide the thoughts of the viewer away from the disappearing skull, and toward a young woman—who will supersede the skull in Poussin's second version?

While painting his first version, Poussin probably did not have the second in mind. But the seeds of the transformation were perhaps already germinating.

Poussin may have consciously thought out the transformation, or it may have resulted from the unconscious workings of his mind. But in either case should one not conclude that the young woman of the second version, who is standing so still (and thus in opposition to the dynamic stance of the three shepherds), is a figure of death, or at least of fate; and that such a flattering guise is appropriate to one who would impose her sovereignty "even in Arcadia"? In contrast to the woman in the first version—a gracious, unassuming companion to the shepherds—the woman in the second displays the lofty impassivity of a mythological figure. She stands haughty and dignified, the implicit source of the words engraved on the tomb; she invites the shepherds to decipher them, and by her mere presence signifies, "In Arcadia too, I am at your side."

One may even imagine the following scenario: she may have just walked onto the group from the right, remaining unseen until she laid a hand on the shoulder of the youngest shepherd, in a gesture of appeasement mingled with force. The shepherd looks back at her but is not surprised at her sudden appearance, for his plastic function is, if I may say so, to establish a link between the young woman and her motto. Thus his face is turned toward her while his hand points to the words, as though to signify their common identity.

If one grants that Poussin saw in Guercino's painting the first stage of a transformation that he would conceptualize and complete, one can understand why, more than any other painting, the Louvre's *Et in Arcadia ego* has prompted the fabulations of philosophers. Father Dubos, Diderot, Delille, the Chevalier de Jaucourt all describe the painting in ways quite removed from reality. It is true that they apprehended the transformation only in its final stage. However, because it was a transformation, it retained sufficient dynamism to be furthered by the viewers themselves. In his description, de Jaucourt, who seems to have been inspired by Dubos, places a recumbent statue of a young girl on the tomb, thus providing what could be yet another stage in the transformation.

It seems more logical to me to interpret the painting as I have than to assume that Poussin reversed the meaning of the Latin motto over the course of several years, and all the more so as Bellori, one of Poussin's friends, provided a commentary of the painting in 1672 with the correct interpretation of the Latin phrase (as pointed out by Panofsky himself). Only in 1685 was it misinterpreted, with Félibien. What is more, how could one account for the extraordinary fame of the work—one of Poussin's most popular, whose chromolithographic reproduction hangs over many a mantelpiece—if it were merely a rural scene with a moralizing message? It draws its powerful attraction from the intimation that the mysterious woman standing by the three shepherds does not belong to this world; that she is the manifestation in this rustic setting of a supernatural presence that, in different guises, always looms in Poussin's landscapes.

4

Though Poussin's *Et in Arcadia ego* is by all accounts the most popular of his paintings, it is *Eliezer et Rebecca* that seems to have inspired the most commentary. No other painting is discussed at such length by Félibien. In the fascinating *Conferences on Painting and Sculpture* of the *Académie royale*, which in my view are far richer than Diderot's chatty *Salons* (Sébastien Bourdon's superb 1669 talk *Light* is exemplary—moreover, a closer look at these *Conferences* reveals that some of Diderot's most famous ideas had already been expressed: the theory of the ideal model, for instance, is presented a century earlier in Gérard Van Opstal's 1667 analysis of the *Laocoön*). In these *Conferences*, Philippe de Champaigne opened up a debate about *Eliezer et Rebecca* in 1668. The debate was taken up again in 1675, then in 1682; in that session, the minutes of the first debate were read and discussed in the presence of Colbert, who was himself a participant.

Several of Poussin's paintings are sublime, but *Eliezer et Rebecca* may be the most exquisite. Each figure is a masterpiece in its own right; so is each group of figures; so is the painting taken as a whole: three levels, each embedded in the other, each raised to the same degree of perfection, so that the work as a whole exudes a particularly rich beauty. The painting unfolds a number of dimensions, each with the same attention to the play of colors and shapes. Contemporaries of Poussin decried his lack of skill with colors. This painting alone would prove them wrong, with its almost raw blue, a favorite of Poussin's. Though deprecated by Reynolds, it is this very blue that instills a particular sharpness in Poussin's palette. Félibien was clearly aware of the importance of color, so much so that he devoted six out of twenty-five pages to it in his analysis of this marvelous work.

Philippe de Champaigne for his part offered a rather static interpretation of the painting. He analyzes various aspects in turn: the representation of action, the ordering of the groups, the deportment of the characters, the distribution of color, and of light and shadow. In his comments on the deportment of the characters, one of his critiques (later to be rejected by Le Brun) seems to me, on close reading, to allow the analysis to progress along a new path:

> In his considerations on the figure of a young girl resting on a vase close to the well . . . M. de Champaigne remarked that Poussin had copied the proportions and the draperies of this figure from antiquities, and thereby remained scrupulously servile to his model. In his talk, he seemed to chastise M. Poussin for being somewhat sterile in his frequent imitation, and went as far as to intimate that he had plundered the work of the ancients.

It is true that this statuelike figure stands out from the whole, but I think it confers a calculated contrast that provides the key to the painting.

Consider it from the perspective of the person who sees it for the first time. The eye is first attracted by the two protagonists standing in the middle foreground, but they have been placed slightly to the right so that the perspective draws one's attention to the busy, compact group of women on the left. The movement in this group contrasts with the stationary mass of the buildings just above them, as well as with the three motionless onlooking women on the right-hand side of the painting. Taken as a whole, the work plays on the opposition between stability and instability, motion and stillness. Does this have any significance?

I am not going to attempt to turn Poussin into an anthropologist. Yet Le Brun, his disciple, explained that the "painter-philosopher" (as they called him at the time) was a discerning and knowledgeable man who "never placed anything in his work without strong reasons, and only painted after lengthy deliberation based on extensive reading and research—and that this rendered his work all the more commendable."

There can be no doubt that before setting to work, Poussin meditated at length on Genesis 24. Though he did not interpret the chapter in the terms of contemporary anthropology, he certainly penetrated its spirit.

Rebecca's marriage was problematic (as Rachel's would be in turn) because it set up a contradiction between what the jurists of the ancien regime would have termed *race* and *land*. On the command of the Almighty, Abraham and his family had left their homeland, Mesopotamian Syria, to settle far to the west. But Abraham was firmly opposed to marrying into the families of the original occupants of his new country, insisting instead that his son, Isaac, should marry a girl of his own blood. As neither he nor his son could leave the Promised Land, he sent Eliezer, his trusted servant, off to his distant kin to bring back Rebecca.

This is the situation illustrated by the painting. In the foreground, a man (the only male) and a woman stand face to face, symbolically representing the coming marriage. The rest of the scene is nothing but women—"race"—and stone—"land." And at one particular spot in the painting, Poussin provides a solution to the opposition, a solution formulated in plastic terms. From the busy group of women on the left, one's glance moves past the two protagonists, who are already calmer, to the still, almost stiff figures on the right, and, in particular, to the woman decried by Philippe de Champaigne as a servile copy from antiquity. This statuelike figure is almost a stone effigy ("Poussin, in his excessive love for antiquity, has lapsed into stone," to quote Roger de Piles) in terms not just of its shape, but also of its uncertain color (one that is quite at odds with all the others). This figure realizes the synthesis between an image that is still human—thus pertaining to race—and the stone pillar—thus close to land—topped with a sphere. The pillar itself, against which the woman is profiled, and with which she is almost fused, suggests a geometrical (even cubist) representation of a woman balancing a water jug on her head, turning what is a precarious balance into something stable; the pillar also replicates on a monumental scale the woman who dominates the group on the left in the same posture of the water carrier (and who is the very image of Rebecca, no doubt intentionally). In this regard, one will note the triangle formed by the jug on her head—unstable—the jug on the ground below her (or even Rebecca's jug)—stable—and the jug placed at midheight on which the statuelike figure leans.

One's eye now turns from the pillar and again to the left. After moving across a natural landscape under a tormented sky (recalling the initial imbalance that has been blown away into the distance) the glance is arrested, this time for good, by the firm-standing buildings on the left. The latter are the symbol of a long-settled land that, through the marriage of Isaac and Rebecca, will eventually be fused with race, itself figured by human forms that resemble each other so closely that they represent less individual women than the female sex in general, which ensures the enduring continuity of the blood.

5

During the debates at the Royal Academy of Painting on *Eliezer et Rebecca*, one question seems to have haunted all participants (and first among them the main speaker, Philippe de Champaigne himself): should not Poussin have included in his painting the camels of Abraham's servant, which are mentioned in the Scriptures? Indeed, it is said that Eliezer knew Rebecca from the care with which she gave them water. This matter led to the most finicky exchange of views: Were not the camels too far from the well to be included in the composition? How large was the herd, and how many could—should—Poussin have painted in the scene (he included a few in a later version)? In their absence, might not the viewer mistake Abraham's servant for a merchant trading jewelry? Or, on the contrary, as Le Brun put it, would not the presence of camels have generated confusion with one of those Levantine traveling merchants who were wont to mount such beasts? Was Poussin right to exclude these odd creatures, which might have distracted the viewer's gaze, from such a lofty scene? Or again, would not the camels' unsightliness have enhanced the splendor of the figures, as Champaigne claimed?

Such casuistry, which inflamed the painters and art lovers of the time, seems ludicrous to us today. We no longer call upon such arguments in our appreciation of a painting. Yet we should keep in mind that for the seventeenth century, the distance between biblical times and antiquity, on the one hand, and the present, on the other, was not thought as great as for us. Try to adopt an ethnographic perspective and translate their arguments into contemporary terms. Would we not face the same problem, when representing recent events? Would we not expect them to be treated truthfully and with respect, and would we not pay great attention to the details?

This is why we have surrendered the representation of recent history to photography and film, under the illusion that they reproduce the events in their reality. Conversely, we no longer feel bound, out of respect for the holy texts "never [to] add nor subtract any parcel of such truths as are taught by the Scriptures." For Poussin's contemporaries, still under the influence of the Renaissance, the historical distance between biblical times, or antiquity, and the present remained contracted and blurred. We, for our part, are more keenly aware of the historical distance, and we compound it with a critical distance.

And yet, artists have long been judged by their capacity to imitate reality to perfection—a criterion that still prevailed in our own culture until recently. The Greeks had a wealth of anecdotes to extol their painters: painted grapes that birds tried to peck at, equine images that horses mistook for their fellow creatures, and a painted curtain that the artist's rival demanded be lifted in order to reveal the picture hidden beneath. Legend has credited Giotto and Rembrandt with the same sorts of feats, and the Chinese and Japanese had very similar myths concerning their own famous painters: painted horses that leave the picture at night to graze and dragons that fly into the air as the artist applies the finishing touch.

In North America, the Plains tribes made a mistake in a similar vein when they first saw a white painter, Catlin, at work. He had drawn one of them in profile; another, no great friend of the first, cried out on seeing the picture that it proved the model was but half a man. A deadly fight ensued.

What Diderot admired most about Chardin was his capacity to imitate reality: "His porcelain vase is real porcelain, real water stands between our eyes and the olives contained in them . . . and his biscuits are there for the eating." A hundred years later the Goncourts echoed Diderot in praising Chardin for having so exactly rendered "the amber-like translucency of the white grapes, the sugary frost on the plums, the dewy purple of the strawberries . . . the fine venulae on the winter apples."

Popular wisdom testifies to the relevance of Pascal's plaint "How vain painting is, exciting admiration by its resemblance to things of which we do not admire the originals!" Even romanticism, though it deems art to represent not nature but the artist's inner passions, poses the same problem, as does contemporary criticism, which considers the work of art as a system of signs. Indeed, trompe l'oeil painting has always reigned supreme, and still does, in the visual arts. When painters believe that they have freed themselves from its empire, it reasserts itself. Take the collage, which is only another kind of trompe l'oeil, but taken one step further, in that it uses material things instead of imitating them. Marcel Duchamp's trajectory provides a most eloquent illustration of this point. He had thought that, by using antithetical devices such as *ready mades* and the intellectual constructions exemplified by his

La Mariée mise à nu or *Le Grand Verre,** he was finally ridding painting of its figurative pretensions. But he ended up devoting his final
years to a secret opus that only came to public knowledge after his
death: it was no less than a three-dimensional diorama to be viewed
through an eyepiece. John Martin himself, the virtuoso of monumental trompe l'oeil, never consented to having his paintings
diminished by this form of presentation, be it two-dimensional.

What gives trompe l'oeil its power of enchantment? The latter
results from the seemingly miraculous coalescence of the indefin-
able and fleeting aspects of the sensible world, as obtained by technical procedures that, after considerable intellectual labor and a
slowly acquired mastery, allow these aspects to be reconstituted
and permanently fixed. "Our understanding revels in imitation as
of something that belongs to it," Plutarch said. Rousseau was opposed to this extremely difficult art form, condemning "conventional standards of beauty whose sole merit lies with the difficulty
overcome." To which Chabanon, his contemporary, rightly
replied: "In the theory of the Arts, it is wrong to pretend that the
difficulty to be overcome counts for nothing; on the contrary, it
plays a considerable part in the pleasure procured by the Arts."

It is not by chance that trompe l'oeil is of considerable importance to still-life painting. It provides manifest proof that inanimate objects too have souls, as the poet says. A piece of cloth or
jewelry; a fruit, flower, or utensil of any kind—all are inhabited by
an inner truth, equal to that of the human face, the preferred object of other genres of painting. One arrives at this inner truth,
Chardin said, through one's feelings, but technical knowledge and
imagination alone can render it. In its own way, and on its own
terrain, trompe l'oeil serves to unite the senses and the intellect.

**The Bride Stripped Bare by her Bachelors; The Large Glass.*

Impressionism renounced trompe l'oeil. Yet contrary to the impressionist creed, the difference between schools of painting does not lie in the opposition between the subjective and the objective, or the relative and the absolute. Impressionism is under the illusion that one can set oneself up permanently where the two meet. The art of trompe l'oeil, however, is aware that advanced knowledge of the object and deepened introspection must each be pursued separately if one is to go beyond the superficial contact between subject and object established at the level of perception and arrive at a synthesis that encompasses each in its entirety.

Hence it is erroneous to believe that photography killed the art of trompe l'oeil. Photographic realism does not distinguish accidents from the nature of things, but places them both on the same level. There is certainly a process of reproduction, but the part played by the intellect is minimal. Though the masters of the genre may have perfected their technique, the latter remains servile to a "thoughtless" vision of the world.

With trompe l'oeil, one does not represent, one reconstructs. This requires knowledge (even of what is not shown) together with reflection. Trompe l'oeil is selective; it does not seek to render everything about the model, nor just anything. It chooses the dusty quality of the grapes rather than some other aspect, because it fits into a system of perceptible qualities formed of the glossiness of a silver or pewter vase (its other qualities ignored), the crumbly character of a piece of cheese, and so on.

With all its technical sophistication, the photographic camera remains a coarse device compared to the human hand and brain, to wit the unsurpassed beauty of early photographs, produced at a stage when the primitiveness of technical means required the artist to throw all his science, time, and will into the balance.

Rather than seeing photography as the death of trompe l'oeil, it would be better to recognize that they possess diametrically opposed virtues. One has only to consider the miserable productions of neofigurative artists who paint portraits or still lifes, not from life but from color photographs they slavishly try to copy. Although they are said to give new life to trompe l'oeil, the opposite is the case.

In the eighteenth century, Father Morellet wrote: "Nature does not bestow beauty on all mothers [or all lovers], and even when it does, their beauty cannot be sustained; sometimes it lasts only a moment." As the term *snapshot* suggests, photography seizes this moment and exhibits it. Trompe l'oeil grasps and displays what was not perceived, or only dimly or fleetingly so, but that, thanks to its art, can now be seen at one's leisure. A basketful of strawberries will never look the same to one who recalls how the seventeenth-century Germans or Dutch, or later Chardin, painted them.

6

———

In Poussin's paintings, the parts are the equal of the whole. Each part is a masterpiece in its own right; each part, by itself, offers as much to the gaze. Thus the painting appears as a secondary articulation of arrangements that have already been determined even in their details. This also holds when the direction is reversed: sometimes, in a painting by Poussin with several figures, one appears by itself like a complete canvas by Corot. The composition of the whole transposes on a larger scale the arrangement of the parts, with each figure being as thoroughly conceived as the sum total. It is no wonder that in his correspondence Poussin, following the practice common to his time, measured a painting's difficulty by the number of figures it contains. Each figure is as challenging as the work as a whole.

What is true for figures also holds for landscapes, whether they depict nature alone or the works of man. The latter are, to be sure, human constructions, but because of their prominence and the meticulousness of their execution (one would think they were inspired by Flemish painting), these constructed landscapes have greater importance and sustain a greater interest than their often tiny denizens, even when they are placed in the foreground. That the inanimate should be made sublime puts man "in his place"— in the moral as well as the common sense of the phrase. Even those paintings that depict giants (*Orion* and *Polyphème**) appear to compose pastoral symphonies where the giants blend into nature more than they dominate it. If one did not know the myth, one might imagine Orion in his downward march, engulfed by the vast expanse of green at his feet.

Ingres clearly saw the moral and aesthetic significance of this reversal: "The immortal Poussin discovered the picturesque soil of Italy. He discovered a new world, like the great navigators Amerigo Vespucci and others . . . he was the first and only one to imprint style on nature as seen in the Italian countryside."

On the same page, Ingres wrote: "Painters of historical topics are the only ones capable of painting beautiful landscapes." Why? Because they do not follow their own instinct first, but instead select in nature what is appropriate to their subject. The so-called theory of natural beauty certainly did not deserve Diderot's sarcasms.

Delacroix wrote in a different, somewhat scornful tone about landscape painting: "Painters of seascapes . . . make portraits of waves, as the landscapists make portraits of trees, of the earth, of mountains, etc. They do not concern themselves enough with the effect on the imagination." One need only substitute the word *perception* for "imagination" to arrive at impressionism. Poussin, however, did not move from nature to subjective emotion (as Delacroix put it "In my paintings, I shall retain only the moving, poetic character of the object"); instead, he aimed at thoughtful selection, fol-

---

Landscape with Polyphemus.

lowed by recomposition. "I have seen him," Félibien relates, "study even stones, lumps of clay and sticks of wood, in order to better represent rocks, terraced plots and tree trunks." It was after one such expedition, which also included the collection of pebbles, moss, and flowers, that he was supposed to have pronounced the famous words "Each of these things will find its place"—or, according to other witnesses, "I have left nothing unheeded."

It was Ingres who said that "flowers should be consulted in order to get beautiful tones for draperies," yet both he and Poussin were deemed poor colorists. The problem is that the word *colorist,* which denotes one who has a sensitivity to colors and their relations, is often given a more technical meaning, referring to the painter who subordinates the choice of colors and their combination to the overall effect he is seeking. Admittedly, Ingres declared:

> Drawing includes three and a half quarters of the content of painting . . . ; smoke itself should be rendered by a line . . . ; drawing contains everything, except the hue . . . ; there has never been a great draughtsman who could not find the right colors to fit the spirit of his drawing.

But have there ever been paintings that, with respect to their coloring, have been more inventive, subtle, and finely tinted than his three Rivière portraits, or those of La Belle Zélie, Granet, Madame de Senonnes, and Madame Moitessier? Or think of the *Baigneuse de Valpinçon, Jupiter et Thétis,* the *Odalisque à l'esclave,* the *Stratonice, Roger Délivrant Angélique,* and the *Bain turc.**

The same misunderstanding was prevalent two centuries earlier. According to the critics of the seventeenth century, the art of

---

**The Bathers of Valpinçon; Jupiter and Thetis; The Odalisque and the Slave; Stratonice; Roger Frees Angelica;* and *The Turkish Bath.*

painting had to reconcile two barely compatible demands: "Aerial perspective" demanded that the thickness of the air be visible when the objects and figures were distant, but at the price of downgrading the colors by several shades, resulting in an overall grayish hue, whereas the search for what was then called the "tout-ensemble" demanded a general tonality, what Charles Blanc in the nineteenth century would call "the orchestration of color, which aims at, above all else, consonance."

It was Charles Blanc who claimed, "Great colorists never render the local tones." To which Delacroix replied: "That is perfectly true. Take this tone, for example [he was pointing, says Blanc, at the grayish, dirty-looking paving stones]; well, if one asked Paul Veronese to paint a beautiful blonde with flesh this very same tone, he would—and the woman in his painting would be a true beauty." Here is a pleasant illustration of the theory of the "tout-ensemble," which Rubens and Van Dyck, each in his own manner, put into practice.

Both Poussin and Ingres are opposed to this point of view. Poussin said of Caravaggio "that he had come into the world to destroy painting"—a phrase that Ingres extended to Rubens. Yet, contrary to what the critics might have written during their lifetimes, both Poussin and Ingres are colorists, and intensely so (in the first sense I have given the word). For they stand almost unequaled in their love of plain hues, almost flatly applied in the case of Ingres, the better to respect "the particular distinguishing tone of each object," and to preserve its individual character and original flavor.

(This is not the only point in common between Poussin and Ingres. The latter's *Triomphe de Neptune*, a scene of bathers at sea, is almost as richly erotic as the *Bain turc*.* Poussin's contemporaries

---

Neptune's Triumph; *The Turkish Bath*.

delighted in the voluptuousness of his female figures, and even wished for more. Later generations were just as aware of their sensuousness, but having turned prudish, took offense and, in one well-known instance, went so far as to mutilate a canvas.)

In order to overcome the contradiction between color and aerial perspective, Poussin and Ingres both chose to consider color as a separate problem, to be treated in its own right once the painting was close to completion. As a result of this procedure they felt free to concern themselves with the true colors. Félibien stressed Poussin's ability to "to give each color, even the brightest, its true place." Thus freed of compromise, drawing and coloring were each able to attain new heights. With regard to coloring, this would even include experiments in dissonance, which, like their equivalent in music, came as a shock at the time, but brought about a tremendous expansion of artistic sensibility.

In the same manner, Japanese prints have established drawing and coloring as two independent processes. In wood engraving, if line drawing is a necessity, brush strokes are out of the question (visible brushwork was despised by Ingres, who called it "an abuse of execution . . . the quality of false talents alone, of false artists alone"). The early prints were almost colorless: barely a few casual touches of orange and green here and there. Later, the brightly colored *nishiki-e* would illustrate in their own manner the character of Japanese "separatism": just as in cooking, there is no mixing of elements—ingredients as well as color tones are all presented in their pure state. One can see to what extent Japanese printmaking was misunderstood by the impressionists, who thought they were emulating it, when (with the compositional makeup excepted) doing just the opposite. Japanese prints (at least those classified as "primitive" by specialists) anticipated Ingres's dictum that "a well-drawn painting is always well painted." Had they understood Japanese printmaking better, the impressionists might have returned to the neoclassicism of a Flaxman or Vien.

As has often been noted, even in the earliest of his portraits (he was twenty-five when he did the three Rivières), Ingres betrayed the influence of Far Eastern art by his separate treatment of drawing and color composition. He was not, however, influenced (contrary to Amaury-Duval's later claims) by Japanese prints, which were not known in Europe around 1805; rather, he must have drawn inspiration from Persian miniatures, as well as from the Chinese paintings that Delacroix accused him of having imitated. Baudelaire too referred to Ingres's work as having "the chequered coloring of Persian and Chinese art." At that time, Asians were deemed masters in the art and science of coloring, and artists studied "Asian ceramists and weavers," who were said—a revealing remark—to "cause the colors to vibrate by superimposing the purest shades: blue on blue, and yellow on yellow."

Kawanabe Kyôsai (1831–1889) was among the last masters of *ukiyo-e*. Although Emile Guimet and Felix Régamey met with him in 1876, it is his 1887 conversation with the English painter Menpes that merits attention. Kyôsai, Menpes reports, was most perplexed at learning that Western painters had models pose for them: take a bird as a model, he said, and it will move about incessantly, and be of no use to the artist. He, for his part, spent days watching a bird. Each time it took, for a fleeting instant, the pose he wished to paint, he would turn away from the model and sketch it from memory, in just a few lines, in one of the several hundred sketchbooks he kept. In the end he had such a clear memory of the pose that he no longer needed to look at the bird to draw it. After a lifetime of such training, his memory had become so acute that he could draw from his head all that he had chanced to observe. For he did not draw from a model present at the time of drawing, but from pictures stored up in his mind.

Ingres seems to have drawn a similar lesson: "Poussin was wont to say that the painter draws his skill from observing things, rather than copying them laboriously [here Ingres merely quotes Felibien]—quite, yet the painter must be gifted with sight." And he goes on to say that the painter should lodge his model inside his head, and become so at home with it that "its nature will dwell in his memory, and thus find by itself its place in his work." Does this not sound like Kyôsai?

I shall not draw the parallel any further. For it is quite obvious that Western and Eastern painters belong to different aesthetic traditions, that they do not share the same vision of the world, and that they use distinctive techniques (the gap would be bridged somewhat if one compared Far Eastern painting with Western painting of the thirteenth and fourteenth centuries). Granted, Ingres sounded like Kyôsai when he advised the painter, "Always have a sketchbook in your pocket, and note down with the fewest strokes of the pencil the objects that strike you, if you do not have time to indicate them entirely." The big difference lies in the fact that the "painter of history" (as Ingres liked to call himself) "renders the species in general," whereas the Japanese artist seeks to grasp being in its particularity and fleeting movement; he is closer, in this respect, to the typically Germanic quest for the fortuitous and ephemeral, as Riegl would have it. Admittedly, Ingres was among the great portrait painters—though he deplored the genre, in which the painter simply depicted an individual, often a common individual, with many faults. Yet I should like to think that the parallels I have drawn provide an explanation—and even, I hope, a justification—for my own personal tastes, which embrace with equal devotion the Northern painters (Van Eyck, Van der Weyden), Poussin, Ingres, and the graphic artists of Japan.

Listening to Rameau

7

In his theory of chords, Rameau stands as a forerunner of structural analysis. By applying the idea of transformation (without, however, formulating it), he divided the number of chords distinguished by the musicians of his time by three or four. He demonstrated that all chords can be generated from their counterparts in the major key by a series of inversions. Structural analysis proceeds in the same way when reducing the number of rules concerning marriage or myth: it reduces several rules to a common type of matrimonial exchange, or several myths to the same mythic armature, subject to different transformations.

How far can this parallel be extended? While perusing old reference works in search of insight into the ideas of an earlier time, I chanced upon the article on Rameau in *Grand Larousse du XIXème siècle*—that most remarkable of dictionaries. I was not to find what I had been looking for, yet a commentary on the opera *Castor et Pollux* caught my attention. The article bears no signature, though it was probably written by Félix Clément, a composer and musicologist, and Larousse's main collaborator in the field. Let me quote:

> In this opera, the *Que tout gémisse* chorus, composed in F minor and immediately followed by *Tristes apprêts, pâles flambeaux,** in E-flat, were much admired. The boldness with which Rameau associated these two pieces, in such very different keys, was an unprecedented success. Following the final chord in F minor, there is a long pause, then slowly the basses take up these three notes in unison: F, A, E; they are immediately succeeded by the ritornello of the aria in E-flat.

To quote Adolphe Adam, "It is of such great simplicity that, on analysis, one is tempted to consider it inane, yet the effect produced by the transposition is truly excellent, and the F, A, E in *Castor et Pollux* were long quoted as a stroke of genius."

Were eighteenth-century audiences, then, in raptures over a modulation of keys that would probably go unnoticed by most listeners today? Rameau's music has little effect on today's audiences; sometimes it even bores them (incidentally, the word *boredom* was used by the reviewers of the *Castor et Pollux* staged at the Aix-en-Provence summer festival of 1991). If this music delighted listeners in the eighteenth century, was it not because it introduced revolutionary innovations that are no longer perceived as such today except by professional musicians and musicologists? But was it not also—and above all—because the audiences of the time knew more about music than we do? Rameau's music, and that of his contemporaries, evokes "less" for us when compared to the music of the nineteenth century,

---

*"With a Plaintive Voice All" and "Sad Attire, Gloomy Lights."

on which we were raised—though, as late as the 1840s, Rameau's music "surprised" Balzac because in it "harmony and melody compete with equal force" (incidentally, this judgment would have appeared naïve to Rousseau, who, a full century earlier, accused Rameau of sacrificing melody to harmony—a criticism that would be repeated by the admirers of Cimarosa in relation to Mozart). But in what evokes less for us, more knowledgeable listeners would have perceived more.

As the lovers of exotic food struggle with chopsticks, they learn the following lesson: the simpler the tool, the more skill it requires. The knife and fork were designed for our forebears, who were still eating boorishly with their fingers. To continue in this vein, could we not say that the music we appreciate—from Mozart and Beethoven to Debussy, Ravel, and Stravinsky—comes to us spoon-fed? Whenever it becomes more learned or sophisticated, the technical comprehension of the piece remains beyond our means; so our favorite works spare us the effort and let us sit back in the comfortable, if passive, position of the consumer.

The eighteenth-century listener's appreciation of music was probably more intellectual and genuine, for he or she was less removed from the composer. Today's music lover may read writings on music of a general character, or the biographies of famous composers. But how many would, in order to improve their knowledge of an opera or concert they were about to attend, feel compelled to consult a treatise on music? Such treatises appear far too arduous to us, even those as approachable as d'Alembert's *Eléments de Musique* (1752), at the time a publisher's success and the topic of many a discussion in the salons.

In snobbish circles, musical knowledge had even become a must. Chabanon, a philosopher of music and musician (I will be referring to him at length in chapters 14 to 17), was amused at the resulting affectations. He wrote of those who, in the company of connoisseurs,

> stud their speech with a few words stolen from academic discourse, while employing them inappropriately. I have heard such ill-trained parakeets praise a piece of music for the richness of its harmony, when the latter was impoverished and sterile, wallowing in the same repeated chords. I have heard some praise a tune for its charming modulations before it ever moved from its principle mode. Those who have not been initiated into an Art cannot be too cautious when adopting a scientific tone to discuss it.

(Chabanon was a gifted polemicist. This may account for the interest Voltaire took in him, though Voltaire was thirty-six years his elder—as reflected in the Ferney correspondence, which, admittedly, dwelt more on theater and poetry than on music.)

Balzac devoted two novels of the *Comédie humaine* to music, *Massimila Doni* and *Gambara,* the latter based on a surprising parallel between musical composition and the culinary arts. Both works fail whenever the inspiration becomes too cerebral, instead of simply being content to "arouse our dormant sensations." Balzac had sought counsel from a musicologist (to whom he dedicated the two novels)—and it is quite striking to see that the listeners and critics of his time still judged a musical piece with particular attention to its mastery of tonality and modulation.

In the course of the nineteenth century, however, musical listening seems to have changed radically. Apparently, it turned into that sort of sensibility criticized by Wagner in his account of a concert consecrated to the works of Beethoven: "Here the conductors, as well as the audience, perceive nothing but sounds (as they would the pleasant sounds of some foreign language)—or else they artificially endow the music with some arbitrary, anecdotal, literary meaning." In his own way Amaury-Duval, Ingres's favorite student, confirmed this sensibility when describing his musical tastes and those of his companions: "Just as some appreciate an art form without prior study or even comparison, we loved all kinds of music indiscriminately, and went unashamedly from operetta to the andante of the *Symphony in A*." It seems to me that the average opera lover or concert goer of today is not very different; the situation may even be worse, as the public authorities would have us confer the same legitimacy on rock music as on the *Ninth Symphony*.

Concerning the current rage for exhibitions of paintings, Edgar Wind, an art historian, writes:

> When such large displays of incompatible artists are received with equal interest and appreciation, it is clear that those who visit these exhibitions have a strong immunity to them. Art is so well received because it has lost its sting. In our time many artists, I think, are aware, although not all are so unwise as to say so, that they address themselves to a public whose ever-increasing appetite for art is matched by a progressive atrophy of their receptive organs.

Wagner's words on the eve of his death, as transcribed by Cosima, suggest something similar relative to the appreciation of music: "Yesterday, when he heard about the popularity of Schumann's *Manfred*, he said, 'They feel about it exactly what they felt about *Tristan*, a sort of dizziness of their sensitivity but there is not a trace of artistic appreciation.'"

Eighteenth-century listeners, on the other hand, were enthused by a daring modulation in three notes that went from one key to one of its relative keys, for they felt a certain complicity with the composer. Musical competence was fashionable then, as the wealth of lengthy and well-informed articles on music in the *Encyclopédie* demonstrates. Educated audiences had read Rameau, d'Alembert, and Jean-Jacques Rousseau. Musical theory was undergoing a revolution, and it received as much publicity as Newton's system (including links postulated between them*). This success was not unlike that of today's best-sellers in astrophysics and cosmology, but with one difference: we are but mere consumers of scientific vulgarization, whereas those who frequented the salons of the eighteenth century where music was played (and who were often musicians themselves) were able to judge more or less as practitioners. The gap between composers and listeners was not as large then as it is today.

---

*In his *Optics*, Newton established a mathematical relationship between the diameters of the multicolored rings produced by the refraction of light, and the different lengths of a monochord which produce the notes of an octave.

8

Adolphe Adam (1803–1856), who composed such well-known works as *Le Postillon de Longjumeau, Le Chalet,* and *Giselle,* was, if I am not mistaken, the author of only two books: *Souvenirs d'un musicien* (1857) and *Derniers Souvenirs d'un musicien* (1859). In the *Larousse,* Félix Clément does not indicate his source, and he does not actually quote from Adam's study on Rameau (published in *Revue contemporaine* and reprinted in *Derniers Souvenirs*); yet Adam hails the modulation in act two of *Castor et Pollux* in almost the same terms. His comments are echoed in H. Quittard's article on Rameau in the *Grande Encyclopédie* (edited by André Berthelot): "His masterpiece, *Castor et Pollux,* was yet another triumph." And to back this up, he speaks of "the boldness of its harmony and the new, unexpected modulations."

(*Castor et Pollux* was indeed a triumph. In Diderot's *La religieuse,* *

---

*The Nun.

a novel begun shortly after the 1754 version of the opera, the heroine hums a fashionable tune, that of *Tristes apprêts, pâles flambeaux, jour plus affreux que les ténèbres*. During the third revival, in 1772, in the press of the crowds some fifteen spectators fainted, and several were rumored to have died. At the time of the next revival, the *Mercure de France* of July 1782 announced that more people attended the opening performance than had ever been seen since the opening of the new auditorium of the *Académie royale de musique*.)

Masson, a twentieth-century musicologist, notes, "The three notes sung by the bass, F, A, and E, which link the chorus in F minor to the monologue in E-flat major, received much notice at the time from musicians and critics."

All the commentators are in agreement. In fact, they are repeating what was written in an anonymous pamphlet of 1773, on the occasion of the opera's third revival, one full century before Adam. In this pamphlet, *Réponse à la critique de l'opéra de Castor et observations sur la musique,** one reads the following:

> These two keys are foreign to each other: the chorus is in F minor third, and the monologue in E-flat, with the three notes given by the bass, going up by a third and down by a fourth—F, A and E—providing the bridge between them. Since then one has often tried to imitate this transition; but as everyone knows, it alone has been praised by famous artists. The noble rhythmic figure played by the bass, which with its quick succession of notes provides the ear so much pleasure, has always been admired as reflecting a talent that belongs to genius alone.

---

*"A Response to the Critique of the Opera *Castor et Pollux*, and Some Observations on Music."

Note that this was written less than twenty years after the 1754 version, in which this transition first appeared.

Rameau wrote two versions of *Castor et Pollux*. The first, which was performed on October 24, 1737, does not contain this modulation. It begins with an ornamental prologue that has little bearing on the opera's action. Act 1 opens—after the murder of Castor, which is not shown on stage—with the chorus *Que tout gémisse,* which is separated from *Tristes apprêts, pâles flambeaux* by a scene, still in F minor. This scene ends on the tonic, and the aria in E flat abruptly opens in the new key. Rameau frequently proceeded in this way, as Masson indicates: "Most of the time, a mere juxtaposition of tonics marks the change in keys . . . only rarely did Rameau attempt more sophisticated transitions."

The remaining scores of the 1737 version are rather barren and disclose almost nothing about the orchestration. It was the 1737 version that Auguste Chapuis took as the basis for his setting for voice and piano: he used the *Complete Works* edited by Saint-Saëns, which gives both versions. The first version was adopted for the revival of the summer of 1991 in Aix, which sought to reconstitute the original instrumentation (as Nicolaus Harnoncourt had attempted earlier, in a recording with the Vienna *Concentus Musicus*).

The second version, first performed on January 8, 1754, is far more dramatic: the prologue has been replaced by an eventful first act, with its festive mood interrupted by a surprise attack, a fight, and the death of Castor. As in the first version, though more logically this time, the following act (now act 2) opens with the mourning of the Spartans and the chorus singing *Que tout gémisse;* but this time, the composer has brought together in immediate succession the chorus and the aria *Tristes apprêts, pâles flambeaux*. The transition from F minor to the aria in E-flat major, in which Télaïre deplores the death of her lover, is provided by the three-note modulation.

I first read this version in its setting for voice and piano by

Théodore de Lajarte. This setting, its composer claims, conforms to the January 1754 revival, in which "*Castor et Pollux* had been so drastically rewritten that it almost no longer sounded like the first, October 24, 1737 version." The famed modulation was included in this setting, but—I was surprised to discover—not in its original form: instead of keeping the F, A-flat, E-flat sequence, Lajarte had written F, A-flat, D natural. The note standing out in the modulation is no longer the tonic, but the leading note in the new key.

On the recommendation of Gilbert Rouget, M. François Lesure, former head librarian of the music department at the Bibliothèque nationale, was kind enough to send me copies of two original scores, one in printed form and annotated by Rameau himself, and the other in manuscript form: the note in question is indeed an E-flat. And it is an E-flat that one hears in the recording of the 1754 version by the English Bach Festival Singers and the English Festival Baroque Orchestra, conducted by Charles Farncombe in January and February 1982 (I was able to procure this recording from *Radio-France* thanks to Didier Eribon).* I would like to express here my debt to all those who helped guide me, a mere layman in the field, through this musicological maze.

But how is one to account for the substitution of notes in Lajarte's score? Did he think that linking the two relative keys with a modulation on the leading note was more in keeping with academic wisdom—fearing that a modulation on the tonic might sound "inane," a fear that Adam had expressed but immediately rejected? In Lajarte's transcription the ritornello to Télaïre's aria no longer seems faithful to the score of 1754, or even that of 1737.

Whatever Lajarte's reasons, I was at this point finally able to put myself in the shoes of the eighteenth-century listener, to hear the fragment as Rameau had actually written it.

---

*It has since been published as two compact disks by Erato, 4509-95311-2.

9

What, exactly, was I hearing? A tonal modulation, to be sure—but if my curiosity had not been piqued by a few musty texts, I would probably have not, as an average listener, been struck by its boldness, let alone its originality. On the other hand, the Spartans' chorus and Télaïre's aria appeared to me as a single block, forming a strangely beautiful whole (though only in the 1754 version). Hence, for me, the significance of the modulation that binds the two halves could not be simply tonal; what was much more important was its rhythmic, metric, and melodic value.

When praising the Spartans' chorus, Adam singled out its color and expression:

> This three-part scale in half-notes, in imitations ... gives forth the richest, most picturesque harmony ... such invention had never been attempted before ... as one can perceive by hearing or reading the piece, it exudes a lofty sadness; but it is impossible

to fully appreciate the emotion sustained by this admirable chorus independent of its actual recital.

The chorus is in F minor, yet it sounds as though the prelude, as well as the orchestral interludes, seeks to undermine, through a series of chromatic descents, the very idea and perception of tonality. And yet, following this chromatic assault, the modulation establishes a small tonal fortress ("It belongs to the fundamental bass," points out the anonymous author of the *Réponse*): its three notes are tonics—the first, in the piece that is just ending; the second (A-flat), in its relative key; and the third is a tonic, both in the ensuing piece (in E-flat) and in the relatives to the other two keys. What is more, following a chorus built entirely out of short intervals, this modulation operates a transition from a chromatic to a diatonic order that, with intervals of up to an octave, reaches its full force in the ritornello of Télaïre's aria. In this sense, the choice of E-flat as the pivot note, which is a half-tone higher than the leading note, serves to prepare the listener for the diatonic intervals; the ternary rhythm prevailing in the aria's accompaniment has also been announced by the three notes of the modulation. Thus the modulation does much more than simply announce a new key: it effects the passage from the chromatic to the diatonic and prefigures, on a reduced scale, the remarkable motif drawn by the bassoons accompanying Télaïre's aria.

It all appears so carefully constructed that one begins to wonder. In the 1737 version, the two pieces were separated by a long scene in the same key as the chorus, which prevented their unity from being perceived. Did Rameau originally conceive of them as a unit, which he then attempted to break up? Or did he only discover the connection afterward and then seek to highlight it in the second version? It would be interesting to know how the specialists would respond to these questions.

All the more so as one must consider another aspect, related to the first. Eighteenth-century listeners, whether or not they were composers (and many music lovers of the time wrote music), were highly sensitive to its technical dimension. But they were also attentive to expression, that is, to the way music conveys a variety of situations and emotions. One listener criticized the *Que tout gémisse* chorus, claiming its beauty was purely conventional, that it was "church music" and completely out of touch with what was happening on stage. To which Gluck rejoined: "That is exactly how it should be, [for it] is truly a burial, *with the body being present*." These were his very words, as cited and underlined by the editor of the July 1782 issue of the *Mercure de France*. (As early as 1773, the author of the *Réponse* had disputed the reputed resemblance between the chorus and church music; he may then have been writing in response to Chabanon, who could have been the author of the following anonymous comments in the *Mercure*: "Suppose that Rameau had stuck the funereal chant from *Castor* to the first section of [Pergolese's] *Stabat,* do you think anything would have been lost?" And in his book, *De la Musique considérée en elle-même et dans ses rapports avec la parole, les langues, la poésie et le théâtre,* Chabanon wrote: "We thus profess that the opening lines of the *Stabat,* sung in very soft voices by the chorus before Castor's grave, would fit the situation to perfection.") Concerning this chorus, Rameau himself wrote that "the abundance of descending chromatic intervals paints the sighs and tears welling up from the deepest sorrow."

Again, Rameau's commentary on Télaïre's aria illustrates his conviction that each technical trait is unequivocally tied to an expressive value. His comments are worth quoting here:

Does one not naturally feel something of the contrition of the actress who is singing *Tristes apprêts . . .* in *Castor et Pollux,* at the moment when the melody descends a fifth, passing from C to F on the final syllable? And does one not feel somewhat relieved as the C returns, on the final syllable of the next two words, *pâles flambeaux**—yet without retaining any trace of the first impression? . . . Substitute a G for the F, and one will soon feel the difference; as long as the note remains the same, the soul will retain its equilibrium and become indifferent to everything, immovable.

Berlioz will take up this argument, claiming that in Télaïre's aria,

each and every note is important, because each note expresses precisely what is required of it. . . . Including the return of the main theme, with its plagal movement from A to the tonic E despite the expected diatonic move from the A, the chord's diminished fifth, down to G; including also the bass, as lugubrious in its gloomy immobility as in its downward progression! Everything conspires to make this aria one of the most sublime pieces in dramatic music.

Rameau himself explained that in this aria he was attempting to paint "the feeling of a mournful, lugubrious pain." Masson, though much closer to us, expresses the same sentiment: "In the monologue sung by Télaïre, the slow, ponderous accompaniment with its drawn-out chords and long pauses, suggests a great sadness and mournful despondency." And his explanation follows that of Rameau: "In the opening notes, the two descending intervals [the perfect fifth and fourth] have something fierce about them, which is accentuated all the more by the division of the octave by the

---

*In fact, the notes are A-flat and E-flat, but "by the method of transposition, the tonic in a major mode is always called C" (see the *Encyclopédie,* under "*Ut*").

subdominant"—the subdominant, according to Rameau, being extraneous to the tonic.

Such unanimous agreement should not cause us to forget that Télaïre's aria was, during the eighteenth century, an object of controversy. In the April 1772 *Mercure* article quoted earlier, the anonymous author (believed to be Chabanon) expressed sharp criticism of the monologue *Tristes apprêts:* "[It] was sublime in its time [but at present] blows a cold wind over the audience . . . we are inwardly frozen with boredom." In his *Éloge de M. Rameau,* a eulogy pronounced after the composer's death in 1764, Chabanon had already made clear his opinion: "Télaïre's mourning song . . . with its touching sadness, is a remarkable recitative, but not a beautiful aria." His anonymous contender rebelled against this judgment. Rameau, he claimed in his *Réponse,* could have added a brilliant accompaniment to Télaïre's aria, but chose not to:

> Rameau handled the orchestra so deftly that the accompaniment, subordinated to the main action, enhances the singing anew, and appears even to add to the scene's gloominess. . . . The actress's impact would have paled before a more powerful and decisive orchestra . . . and it is the actress, not the orchestra, who should address the audience.

For me, the opposite is the case. Far from the monologue's "appearing to be dependent on the chorus," the chorus seems to me to prepare the way for the orchestral part of the monologue that brings it to its logical conclusion. What eighteenth-century listeners (with the exception of Chabanon, who praised Gluck, in Renaud's monologue in act 2 of *Armide,* for having confided the main line of the melody to the symphony, and the expression of words to the orchestra), what Rameau himself, as well as Berlioz and Masson, perceived as being foregrounded, I see, by contrast, as background, and what they perceived as background is for me foregrounded.

I believe that I am not the only one today who remains largely unmoved by Castor's death, the Spartans' mourning, or Télaïre's despair. We have grown more demanding about the expression of feeling. Different kinds of music touch us, music like *Don Giovanni*, *Tristan und Isolde*, *Carmen*, *Tosca*, or *Pelléas et Mélisande*. To me, the ritornello to Télaïre's aria is devoid of expression, like "one of those arrogant accompaniments that appear to mock their subject by failing to have any palpable relation to it," as decried by one of Rameau's contemporaries, quoted by Masson. The only difference is that what he condemned is the very aspect of this accompaniment I value: it develops and justifies, within a long phrase, the form and content of the modulation that had provided its anticipatory sketch.

The ritornello and the orchestral phrases that follow, because I find them indifferent to human feelings, affect me in quite a different way. They sound as though they belong to a different world, or a foregone age—imagine a cadence by Bach taken up and modified by Stravinsky (indeed, the impression left by the bassoons brings to mind Stravinsky's *Octet for Wood Instruments*). The language of the orchestra is external to the dramatic action on stage. As a language, it cannot be said to express anything—its significance is strictly musical.

One sees the orchestral prelude to Télaïre's aria, which is formally constructed on the model of the modulation that prepares it, as a development of this self-same modulation. It proceeds, in the image of the latter, by means of triads of notes (completed by the bass) that form chords, each of the same length, slowly played in arpeggio. And it revolves around the chord of E-flat and its inversions—beginning with this chord, then moving away, only to return to it at the end. By way of this progression (a surprising one, given the wide intervals), this austere, rigorous composition succeeds in transforming the extremely chromatic chorus of the Spartans into an equally extreme diatonic mode. Far from providing a mere transition between two keys, as Rameau's contemporaries would have had it, the modulation reveals a complex formula designed by the composer to realize, in almost architectural fashion, a plan conceived according to several dimensions.

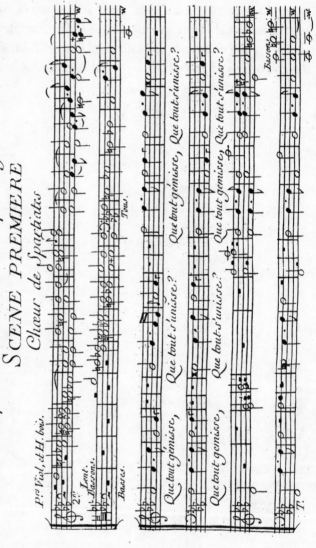

Jean-Philippe Rameau, *Castor et Pollux*, 1754 version

Castor et Pollux.

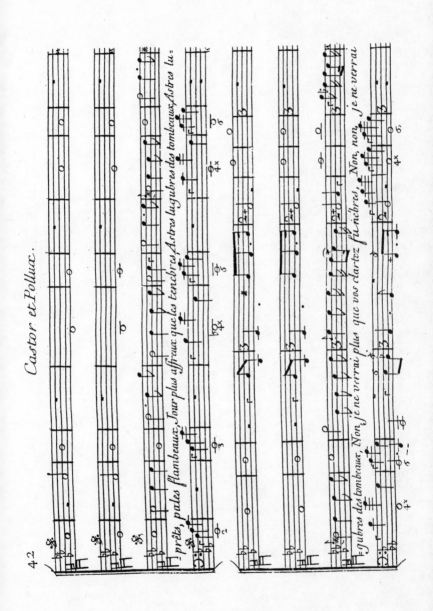

Castor et Pollux.

Reading Diderot

10

When Diderot demanded that the artist be endowed with "two basic qualities . . . morality and perspective," he was approaching painting in the same way that his contemporaries approached music: "There is both a technical and moral side to the imitation of nature"; "The artistic fire is of two kinds: that of the soul and that of the craft." Today, we no longer pay equal attention to the form and the subject matter. We are less interested in what a painting represents than in the way the painter chose to represent it. With the figurative element moving to the background, the painting's subject matter loses its importance, though a minimal relation to reality must be maintained, if painting is not to lose itself completely in the wreckage of nonfigurative art.

Although interest in painting's moral qualities has disappeared, the intellectual interest remains intact. (The absence of the moral side is not, one should add, without its negative implications: a nonbeliever will not be as moved by an artist's religious painting—

however sublime—as by his more secular work. For were nonbelievers to question their judgments, they would be unable to attribute any moral value to the religious paintings, which to them do not really represent anything. Art's moral dimension still exerts an influence, even on those who think they have freed themselves of it, but in reverse, as it were.)

Thus, unlike the formalists, I am not one to underestimate the capital importance of Panofsky's iconographic and iconological analyses—far from it. Nor would I, to take but one example, deny the interest of Wind's commentary on Botticelli's *Primavera;* indeed, I am tempted to push his analysis a little further. I would suggest that Castitas, one of the three Graces, is not just turning her eyes toward Mercury; she is on the verge of being hit by Cupid's arrow (and Wind was the first to see this) and will fall in love with Mercury, though he, absorbed by celestial matters, seems not to notice her. Will her love be unrequited, or returned, but in a restrained manner? In either case, the kind of love pictured on the left-hand side of the painting is inversely symmetrical to that on the right, with its show of blatantly physical passion, as represented by the couple formed by Zephyr and Chloris. In the movement from the one couple to the other, the active and passive polarities are also reversed between the sexes.

Whatever the hypothesis, the subject matter is of intellectual interest. It presents itself to the artist as a problem requiring a solution, by virtue of the semantic constraints it imposes (in terms of the "subject's treatment"). To these constraints are added those resulting from the pursuit of harmony in its formal sense—the arrangement on the canvas of lines and colors that, in themselves, are aesthetically pleasing. It is through the encounter of these two sets of requirements that the work achieves a superior level of organization. What operates as a term in the one system becomes a function in the other, and vice versa.

In his *Essai sur l'origine des langues,** Rousseau sketched out a theory of painting to illustrate his conception of music. He viewed the two arts as in a birefringent crystal: for painting, drawing is on one side, coloring on the other; for music, melody on the one side, harmony on the other. As Starobinski puts it: "Rousseau postulates that the opposition between melody and harmony pair is homologous to that between drawing and coloring." Nonetheless, music and painting do differ: "Each color is absolute and independent while each sound is, for us, only relative, distinguished only by comparison." (But sounds do exist independently, like colors, provided one defines them by their number of vibrations. Conversely, in painting, the intrinsic properties of colors are subordinated to the relations the artist establishes between them. Depending on whether he was speaking of painting or music, Rousseau sometimes spoke of things, and sometimes of the relations between things.)

While pursuing his comparison between the two arts, Rousseau at times almost appears to have foreseen, and to have condemned, the idea of a nonfigurative art:

> Imagine a country in which no one has any idea of drawing, but where many people who spend their lives combining and mixing various shades of color are considered to excel at painting [though they limit themselves to] a primitive beauty, which does not really express anything but merely plays with different shades, filling the canvas with brilliant colors and endless gradations without ever drawing a line.†

**Essay on the Origin of Languages.*

†The latter half of this quotation is missing from the English translation of *The Essay*. [Translator's note.]

Claude Lévi-Strauss

One would remain at the level of pure sensation, or else, "the power of progress would lead to experiments with the prism," and one would end up with a doctrine claiming that the art of painting consists entirely in learning about and putting into effect "the exact relations that exist in nature." A striking apologue, as it prefigures in caricature form the impasse reached by the early impressionists, and the way out of it devised by Seurat.

This discussion appears to have been inspired by Abbé Batteux's work *Les Beaux-Arts réduits à un même principe,* published in 1746 (and, incidentally, outrageously plundered by Diderot under cover of criticism). I quote:

> All music must have a meaning. . . . What would one say about a painter who was content to throw bold lines and bright masses of color onto his canvas without seeking the least resemblance to any known object? The same observation naturally applies to music. . . . Though the calculation of its tones and the geometry of its chords be unparalleled in their exactness, should the music, despite these qualities, be devoid of meaning—then it can only be compared to a Prism that produces the most beautiful colors without ever forming a picture. It would sound, as it were, like a chromatic clavichord that produces colors and transitions that may please the eye, but would surely bore the mind.

Elsewhere Rousseau is bolder, offering more original considerations on the role of convention in aesthetic perception: "Even imitation is arbitrary to some degree." This is true for harmony, whose so-called laws are the result of a series of approximations and please us not because of their truth but as a result of custom. The same applies to painting: "If the viewer refuses to play the game, but simply looks at the painting as it is, he will misjudge all the relations, and they will all seem wrong." In the painting's tone, its play of colors, and certain parts of the drawing, "there is a more arbitrary touch than one thinks, and . . . even the art of imitation is conventional to some degree."

Then comes the following, rather surprising passage:

Why are painters afraid to attempt new kinds of imitations, ones that have naught against them but their novelty, and which still fully belong to art's domain? For example, see how easily they can make a plane surface look as though it were in relief; why then hasn't someone tried to give relief the appearance of a plane surface? If they can make a flat ceiling appear like a vault, why not make a vault appear flat? They will object that in relief, as opposed to plane surfaces, the shadows move depending on one's line of vision. But let us remove this difficulty, and ask the painter to paint a statue so that it will seem flat and bare, all of one shade, without any lines, as though perceived in but one light and from a single line of vision.

As in anticipation, Rousseau may have perhaps here discovered one of cubism's secrets. I do not know whether a cubist ever colored a statue, but whenever one of them paints a statue on canvas, its volume is destroyed, its shape flattened, and the shadows are suppressed or replaced by shades of color.

When speaking of painting, Rousseau distinguished between the sensual pleasure provided by color, whose value is purely decorative, on the one hand, and the knowledge of its physical laws, which adds nothing to the art, on the other. The same dualism appears in music when it is reduced to harmony: one is forced to choose between either a purely sensual appreciation of the sounds or the application of laws that will result in an intellectual music incapable of giving any pleasure.

As regards music's or painting's other dimension—drawing in the one case, melody in the other—Rousseau gave them a descriptive function: "It is imitation alone that raises them to the rank of [the fine arts]." By judging drawing in terms of its anecdotal value, Rousseau takes us far from Ingres's conception of drawing as "the very integrity of art"—that by which the work of art attains its compositional rigor and internal balance. Rousseau, along with Diderot, split the fine arts into technique and figuration, without seeing that they lie entirely in the space between the two.

II

In each of his paintings, Poussin tells a story. His contemporaries admired above all his ability to create an abundance of characters in order to produce a more detailed account. Nothing, however, is further from the anecdote, for—to use the terminology of linguistics—Poussin's paintings are organized on a paradigmatic axis, and not syntagmatically. Concerning La Manne,* he wrote:

> I have found the compositional distribution ... and the natural stances, which allow one to see how famished and miserable the Jewish people were, as well as the utter joy in which they now find themselves, as well as the great admiration, the respect and reverence they feel for their legislator.

Poussin had gathered all the main elements of the story onto his canvas, but without turning them into a temporal succession of events.

---

*Gathering of the Manna.

Claude Lévi-Strauss

In *Pyrame et Thisbée*,* a painting in the Frankfurt Museum, Poussin depicts a storm, but the still waters of the pond seem to belie the turbulence of the trees shaking in the wind. Just as he claimed that the various movements animating the figures in the painting "express their character according to the weather," so the different moments of the storm have been brought together: the storm unleashed, but with the lull before the first peal of thunder in a darkening sky. This is typical of the way Poussin juxtaposes different elements (it can already be perceived in *La Mort de Germanicus*†) and is the very opposite of the unfolding of a narrative.

The same goes for *Le Judgment de Salomon*‡ at the Louvre. There is nothing in the story (at least not in the biblical text, I Kings 3:16–27) that would justify placing the dead child before the king: he is dead, everyone is agreed, and there is no going back on the matter. To Poussin, however, it is important that all the elements of the story should be there simultaneously, even if they may not have coincided in time. And just as medieval statuary associated each saint with his or her distinctive trait, so Poussin represented the bad mother in accordance with her definition as the child's true mother: the child lies in her arms (providing Poussin with the opportunity for a marvelous arrangement of colors, what with the woman's bilious complexion, the livid skin of the little corpse, the cloak's dark red and olive green, a harmony that would have been impossible to achieve if those tones had to be shared between the two women). Strict observance of the temporal order must not impede the pictorial harmony. While speak-

---

**Landscape with Pyramis and Thisbe.*

†*The Death of Germanicus.*

‡*The Judgment of Solomon.*

72

ing of *Frappement du rocher*,* Poussin claimed this liberty for the painter: "sufficiently well informed as to what is permitted . . . regarding the things he wants to represent—which things may be taken and considered as they are or as they ought to be."

Poussin's contemporaries were just as aware of the problem as he was and, following his example, would not let it stand in their way. When, in a talk on *La Manne* given before the Académie royale de peinture, Le Brun expressed unreserved praise for the painting, someone objected that Poussin ought not to have represented the Israelites in such an extreme state of misery, "for when the manna fell in the desert, the people had already received the godsend of the quails." Le Brun replied that what is appropriate to history does not apply to painting: "As the painter has but a single moment in which to gather all that he wants to paint, in order to represent what happened at that particular time, he may have to include many an earlier incident so that his subject-matter becomes clearer." Félibien too distinguished the historian, who "presents whatever actions he pleases in succession," from the painter, who must "join together various events that occurred at different times."

In this as in other matters, the eighteenth century sometimes appears somewhat reactionary—but then, for the empirical, rationalist spirit to blossom, the stiffening of an increasingly ponderous academicism may have been necessary. At any rate, Diderot did not allow the painter the same latitude as Poussin, Le Brun, and Félibien: "If part of the composition refers to the moment before, or the moment after, he has transgressed the law of unity [of Time in Painting]."

In his article "Encyclopédie," Diderot took up this matter

Moses Striking Water from the Rock.

again, and in an attempt to overcome the difficulty, sketched out an interesting theory. Though "the painting is permanent, it depicts only an instantaneous state," and as such presents nature as a series of discontinuous snapshots: "Produce as many of these figures as you will, there will always be some interruption." Painting thus points to a very general philosophical problem, which the theory of numbers had already confronted: "How to measure a continuous quantity with a discrete quantity?"

Now language, Diderot continues, presents an analogous condition, for there are "delicate nuances in its expression that necessarily remain indeterminate"; and from this it follows that, because "language cannot be made fully intelligible," the encyclopedist can never complete his project and transmit all knowledge.

Nonetheless, there is in language, in contrast to painting, a middle term: the root words. As these are far fewer in number than the words derived from them, they reveal a continuity among different discrete words from the same family; relative to the latter, root words represent an intermediary level that has no equivalent in painting.

Thus it is through *invariance* that the antinomic character of the continuous and the discrete may be surmounted. Yet in his attempt to compare painting and language, Diderot stopped midway. One might have expected him to have examined the notion of invariance in relation to the problems specific to painting. But instead he seems to have credited the paintings of Greuze with having already resolved them: "Here is the thing as it must have taken place!" he exclaimed in his 1759 *Salon*, referring to *L'Accordée de village*.* Nowhere, however, does he appear to have tried to understand, in terms of Greuze's style or principles of composi-

---

The Village Bride.

tion, the character of this invariance. In fact, Diderot's enthusiasm for Greuze was due to other considerations.

It is my belief that this enthusiasm was not unlike that experienced at a later date for the invention of moving pictures, even among devotees of the best painting (didn't Diderot, in his time, admire Chardin?). Greuze invented something similar: he depicted the fleeting moment with such realistic, painstaking means that one had the illusion that it was lasting, if only because of the amount of time required to inspect the painting's details. This had already been achieved in literature by Richardson:

> His stage is the real world in which we now live, the actions are true to nature, the actors live and breathe; they are the people we meet in society, and the incidents that befall them are such as might happen in any civilized country. . . . Unless he had this skill the illusion would be but momentary, and there would be left on my mind only a feeble and passing impression.

What Diderot admired in Richardson and Greuze was, therefore, precisely what would later be demanded of the cinema:

> You have often seen outbursts of passion, but you could not understand all the hidden meanings in the tones of the voice or the facial expressions. Each passion has its own mode of expression, and these different expressions follow each other on the same countenance without it ceasing to be the same face. The art of the great poet or painter is to make you conscious of some quickly passing mood that had escaped your observation.

Could there be a better description of what we see as the function of the closeup? In the same vein, what Diderot admired in Joseph Vernet was his proclivity, to speak somewhat anachronistically, for the "western," that is, his "infinitely artful way of

Claude Lévi-Strauss

interlacing movement and rest, light and gloom, silence and noise."

The history of art sometimes resembles an accordion. With his "necessarily lengthy passages," Richardson stretched out as literature what Greuze's instantaneous cinema compressed into the space of a canvas (though the latter may take a long time to describe, as in Diderot's *Salons*). In its turn, the cinema, which (like painting) works with images, will multiply the latter in order to stretch out time—just as literature does with words.

12

In the opening lines of his article "Beau" (On Beauty) published in 1751 in volume 1 of the *Encyclopédie*, Diderot claimed he was going to settle the question that had eluded all his predecessors, that concerning the nature of beauty. In fact, he repeated an old philosophical idea, which had been resurrected in Rameau's theoretical writings by being applied to music—the idea that beauty lies in the perception of relations. But then the question is, What kind of relations?

In his concern not to separate the abstract from the concrete, the form from the content, and the idea from the thing, Diderot saw the notion of a "relation" as an abstraction by the understanding from an experience that is so common that "there is no other notion—except that perhaps of existence—more familiar to men." But if the notions of relation and existence are coterminous, and if, as a consequence, everything in nature can be perceived in terms of relations, which of these relations serves to ground our sense of beauty? What distinguishes these latter relations from all the others?

On two occasions, Diderot attempted to answer this question. In his *Lettre sur les sourds et muets,** which he wrote at the same time as his article "Beauty," he outlined his theory of "hieroglyphics," according to which poetry has the power of speaking as well as representing things: "At one and the same time, things are grasped by the understanding, seen by the imagination, and heard by the ear." Thus poetic discourse is like a "tissue of hieroglyphics piled one on top of the other." He drew his illustrations from various sources in ancient as well as modern poetry and analyzed them in both phonetic and prosodic terms. Most of his observations could be readily accepted today as starting points for the structural analysis of these same works.

His was indeed a very modern conception of poetry—but was it Diderot's alone? One has noted that it already existed in Batteux's writings, but this is not the half of it. Throughout his *Lettre sur les sourds et muets,* Diderot engaged in ferocious polemics against Batteux. Yet even as he claimed to have triumphed over his adversary by demonstrating that "syllabic, as well as periodic harmony, beget a type of hieroglyphics specific to poetry," he was doing no more than taking up Batteux's own theory of "the three harmonies." Indeed, the first two harmonies are presented in the same order, and the third, the one proper to poetry, differs in name only, being called "artificial" by the one and "accidental" by the other.

Diderot was so receptive to other people's ideas that he often thought that he had had them first. He would then, in all good faith, reproach them for not having thought in his terms and

---

Letter on the Deaf and Dumb.

credit them with notions that he had himself professed before having read them. Such intellectual sleights are not unknown today.

I am not claiming that Abbé Batteux was a great thinker. Yet his central idea, that art has as its sole aim to imitate "nature in its beauty," was rebutted by Diderot with a rather silly argument: a painter, when depicting a picturesque cottage scene, will prefer to set it near "a venerable, gnarled oak, with knotted branches, and which I should cut down if it grew near my door." But Batteux had countered this argument in advance by explaining how objects that are not pleasing in nature can be made agreeable by art:

> In Nature, they lead us to fear our impending doom; by showing us a real danger, they are the source of a powerful emotion. But as the emotion is by itself pleasant, even as the reality of the danger may be quite the opposite, it is a matter of dissociating the two aspects of the same impression. This is precisely what Art manages to do. By giving us the spectacle of what we fear while simultaneously displaying its own artificial nature, Art reassures us and instills a pleasant emotion free of any disturbing admixture.

Several years after his *Lettre sur les sourds et muets* (and at a time when he did not believe that his theory of hieroglyphics could be applied to painting—or rather, his views on this matter were contradictory), Diderot, in his 1763 *Salon*, attempted to break new ground. The colors in a painting, he wrote, do not replicate those of the model, but are homologous to them: "The supreme magic consists in approaching nature and having everything lose or gain while preserving its proportions." Painting is not a matter of imitating, but of translating. And yet once again his arguments fall short, and a few pages later, Diderot admits, "We do not understand anything about this magic." In his 1767 *Salon* nothing remains of the theory of hieroglyphics, if not the idea of "an art that

is no more conventional than the impressions left by a rainbow";
he thus contents himself with a mysterious correspondence between ideas and sounds, which he reduces to sense impressions
without understanding that it is of a primarily intellectual nature.

In order to avoid such conceptual pitfalls he would have had to
recognize that beauty cannot be reduced to the mere perception
of relations—for all objects are apprehended in such terms. What
makes an object beautiful is the fact that these relations are themselves related in turn, giving them a greater density. But Diderot
could accept only simple relations and shunned complexity. The
beautiful object, however, weakens or breaks with the simple relations that connect the different objects of daily experience, and to
which it is tied as one object among others. One takes note of this
effect, or even assists it, by setting off the art object from its sur-
roundings. Poussin was clearly aware of this requirement when he
asked that his painting *La Manne* be "embellished with a bit of or-
nate framing . . . so that the eye, as it considers all the elements of
the painting, does not stray onto a neighboring object that might,
if mixed in with the things painted, interfere with the scene and its
composition."

Thus an increase in the relations internal to the work of art at
the expense of those it maintains with the world without serves to
extend its power. That these relations are related to each other sets
the work apart as an independent entity. Kant's definition of the
work of art remains definitive: an (internal) finality devoid of any
(external) end; in other words, an absolute object.

Diderot's aborted attempts were largely due to that impatience
that marred many an eighteenth-century thinker when confronted
with the demands of experience (despite their interest in the writings of Bacon). They sought out experience avidly, but should it
be lacking, they would not hesitate to make it up; and if they felt
they were losing their bearings, they would fall back into abstrac-

tion. On two occasions, Diderot understood that questions of aesthetics can only be answered when dealing with concrete cases. The first was in his "hieroglyphic" analysis of several lines of Greek, Latin, and French poetry; yet the original idea was not his, and the analysis did not extend beyond matters of sound and meter. The second occasion involved some cogent reflections on Chardin, which he seemed to have forgotten when considering other painters. But let us be fair: he was not unaware of his own shortcomings, and in his article "Beauty" he confronted them directly. Yet how did he envision overcoming them? In a purely negative manner, by listing all the cases in which people perceive relationships they incorrectly believe to be aesthetic. Nowhere did he attempt to define the nature of truly aesthetic relations: that is to say, he left the heart of the matter rather vague.

In fact, Diderot was unable to surmount (by reflection on concrete cases, which requires greater assiduity) the antinomy between the idea and the thing, the senses and the intellect; as a consequence, the article was ultimately a failure. The antinomy would continue into the *Salons* (though here he was faced with particular objects) if in the somewhat reduced form of the opposition between the work's moral and technical dimensions. Depending on his mood, the time of day, or the painter he was commenting on (Greuze or Chardin) he would oscillate between those two poles, but without being able to bring them together, or to perceive that the essence of art lies in between.

13

Kant gave definite form to the idea that aesthetic judgment had a place in between judgments of taste and judgments of reason, being subjective like the former while claiming to be universally valid like the latter. The discovery of fractals reveals, it seems to me, another aspect of this intermediary space, one that concerns not just aesthetic judgment, but the objects on which such judgment bestows the status of a work of art.

Though it requires practice to spot them, fractals are extremely common in nature and often elicit an aesthetic response in us. Are these objects not "intermediary," and in a double sense? First, in that their reality lies, as it were, between the line and the plane; second, in that the algorithms that produce them—the repeated application of a function to its successive products—must have a screening device for distinguishing or eliminating some of the many effects that result from the calculations (depending on whether or not they fall within the field, are odd or even, are on the left or right, or according to some other criteria).

When these calculations are represented graphically or acoustically, fractals appear to illustrate, relative to painting, for example, the most varied forms of what I shall call, to keep things simple, decorative art. Depending on the method of calculation, the initial values chosen, and the employment of complex or real numbers, one has the impression of being faced with different recognizable styles: Oriental designs, art nouveau, Celtic art or its Irish legacy. (It is striking that Celtic patterns are also the product of a screening device: the artist traces numerous intersecting circles with a compass, but retains only some of the arcs of the circles thus traced, while erasing the others.) One hesitates to find too precise a resemblance in some of the calculations' results; still one has to acknowledge that they correspond to styles that have, or at least could have, existed.

Fractals can also be employed in music. Transcribed in terms of the lengths of the notes or the intervals, the calculations produce a music that can also be characterized as decorative, and from which one should not expect anything more than a tolerable acoustic ambiance.

What gives these results a certain piquancy is that a great painter (one who was also a great lover of music) happened to have perceived, on the basis of sense experience alone, the reality and nature of fractals (discovered, along with their mathematical theory, in 1975 by Benoit Mandelbrot) and expressed them in modern terms. In his *Journal,* dated August 5, 1854, Delacroix wrote the following (which he claimed to have transferred from a marginal note written in the forest on September 16, 1849, in one of his sketchbooks):

> Nature is singularly consistent with herself: at Trouville, at the seaside, I drew some fragments of rock in which the accidents of

the form were so proportioned as to give, on the paper, the idea of an immense cliff; all that was lacking was an object suited to establish the scale of size. At this moment, I am writing alongside a big anthill, partly the result of small accidents in the surface of the ground at the foot of a tree, and partly due to the patient work of the ants; there are slopes, and parts that overhang and form little gorges, through which the inhabitants go back and forth with a busy air, like the little people of a little country, which the imagination can magnify in a moment. What is only a molehill, I can see at any time as a vast expanse cut across by precipitous rocks and steep declivities, because of the tiny size of its inhabitants. A fragment of coal or of flint or of any other stone may present in reduced proportion the forms of immense rocks.

At Dieppe I noticed the same thing in the rocks at the water level which the sea covers at every tide; among them I saw gulfs, arms of the sea, frowning peaks suspended above abysses, valleys which by their windings divided up a whole country that showed the accidents we observe about us. The same thing is true as to the waves of the sea, which are divided, themselves, into little waves, again subdividing, and individually presenting the same accidents of light and the same drawing. The great waves of certain seas, those of the Cape for example, which are said to be half a league wide at times, are composed of a multitude of waves, among which the greater number are as small as those that one sees in a garden pool.

I have often noticed, when drawing trees, that a given branch taken separately, is a little tree in itself: for one to see it so it would be sufficient if the leaves merely had the right proportion.

What is astonishing about this text is not just the examples chosen: the seacoast or the tree will become the classic example utilized by the theory of fractals. Delacroix stated with perfect clarity the distinctive property of fractal objects, which, as we know, is that they have the same invariant structure whatever their scale. Or, to use different terms: The part, whatever its size, whether large or small, has the same topology as the whole. To limit myself to a single example, the fractal character of a musical composition results from the fact that the relation between a small number of contiguous notes is repeated unchanged when those fragments are compared with more extensive passages from the same piece.

This sort of construction can be observed in the work of the great masters. Already Balzac noted that "in Beethoven the effects are, so to speak, distributed in advance . . . the orchestral parts in Beethoven's symphonies follow orders given in the general interest and subordinated to admirably well conceived plans." A contemporary musicologist, Charles Rosen, explains the same matter in terms that could almost be borrowed from the language of the theory of fractals:

> This is perhaps Beethoven's greatest innovation in structure; the large modulations are built from the same material as the smallest detail, and set off in such a way that their kinship is immediately audible. . . . One has the feeling that one is *hearing* the structure.

A little later he comes back and speaks of how "the most typical ornamental device is turned into an essential element of large-scale structure."

However, as already noted, fractal algorithms do not have the ability to engender, whether in painting or in music, more than those minor genres I have called decorative—even if, in terms of their refinement and complexity, fractals often exceed, relative to painting at least, anything actually created by decorators. A large gap separates these often fascinating objects from an authentic painting or piece of music. The distance is, in fact, insurmountable. But does this, in principle, have to be the case? In this regard,

one might note that the screening mechanisms necessary to gener-
ate fractals present an analogy with those implemented in stages by
the sense organs and nerve centers, which transmit to the brain
only some of the peripheral impressions they register.

If it is so that the brain abstracts invariant properties out of
these primary givens (but inflected by experience, individual history, and so on), could not the work of art then be the result of a
feedback from the cerebral schema projected onto the work,
which thereby fuses the thought object and sense impression?

Speech and Music

14

Some sixty years ago Jakobson emphasized that

> in linguistic terms, the individuality of music, as opposed to
> poetry, lies in the fact that its totality of conventions (langue,
> after Saussure's terminology) is restricted to the phonological
> system, without any distribution of phonemes according to
> the etymology and therefore without a vocabulary.*

Music does not have words. There is nothing between the
notes—which can be called sonemes (since like phonemes they
have no meaning in themselves, but only consequent to their
combination)—and the phrasing (however defined). There can be
no question of the musical equivalent of a dictionary.

Rousseau sometimes appeared to suggest the opposite: "A

---

*The English translation of the original German mistakenly substitutes the word *vocal*
for "vocabulary." [Translator's note.]

dictionary of selected words is not a sermon, nor is a collection of concordant chords a piece of music." But chords, even "concordant" ones, are not comparable to words. More than anyone else, Rousseau was aware that notes cannot really be distinguished from chords. Each sound is in itself a chord, for "it is accompanied by all its harmonically concomitant sounds"—an argument that Rousseau would turn somewhat maliciously against Rameau: "Harmony is futile since it can already be found within the melody. It does not add to the melody, but duplicates it." Batteux had made the same point even more vigorously: "Even in Nature a simple cry of joy contains the basis of chords and harmony."

This relation will be confirmed by nineteenth-century acoustic science: "Musical sounds are by themselves already partial chords and . . . conversely, under certain conditions, chords can represent sounds." If chords and sounds are so closely related that they sometimes—perhaps always—fuse, then there can be nothing between these and the musical phrasing that resembles the intermediary organizational level that in articulate speech is constituted by words.

Does this also apply to music different from our own, to traditional or exotic music, in which the basic elements, as in Japanese music, are not notes but rhythmic or melodic cells, "the minimal units common to all composers and players"? Even here, one finds nothing akin to words. These units are actually "miniphrases," comparable to the fixed expressions employed by bards and other popular singers and defined by specialists as groups of words "regularly employed under the same metrical conditions to express a given essential idea"—akin, then, to phrasing, even if the latter be idiomatic.

Different peoples speak and have spoken thousands of mutually unintelligible languages, but they can all be translated because they all possess a vocabulary that refers to a common, universal experience (though each language carves it up differently). This is impossible in music, for lacking words it possesses as many languages as composers and perhaps, ultimately, as compositions. Musical languages are, relative to each other, untranslatable, though conceivably they could be transformable—even if this has not, or has hardly been attempted.

In the course of a conversation with Wagner, Rossini is said to have declared: "Who, then, when an orchestra is unleashed, could pinpoint the difference in the description of a storm, a riot, a fire? . . . always convention!" I will grant that an uninformed listener cannot say that it is the sea in Debussy's composition of the same name, or in the overture of *Le Vaisseau fantôme*. One needs a title. But once the title is known, one visualizes the sea on hearing Debussy's *La Mer* and smells its exhalation when listening to *Le Vaisseau fantôme*.

Rossini's response to the problem of imitation is less than satisfactory. The thoughts of a number of almost forgotten eighteenth-century thinkers appear, in this regard, more profound. Michel-Paul-Guy de Chabanon (1730–1792), a violinist and composer, as well as a philosopher, claimed, along with the abbé André Morellet (1727–1819), that music does not imitate our sense impressions nor, strictly speaking, express our feelings. Music, understood as melody alone, cannot render anger or rage. When dramatizing the anger of Achilles, Gluck stifled the voice under some sixty instruments: "Anger is an emotion that cannot be sung." Still the problem of imitation troubled Morellet. He was willing to grant a place for imitation provided that it was imperfect—thus, paradoxically, giving imitation an advantage over nature (the musical rendition of the nightingale's song is more pleasing than its reproduction by mechanical means). Chabanon, in turn, wondered: "Why must poetry, painting or sculpture provide faithful images, and music unfaithful ones? If music is not an imitation of nature, then what is it?" The question, says Chabanon, is misleading, for the ear, like sight and smell, has its own immediate pleasures, which can be enjoyed as such independently of all imitation.

Sometimes, however, music appears to have meaning for the listener. Chabanon explained this, again in agreement with Morellet, in terms of the analogies established between different feelings and the impressions produced by the music. Music acts directly on the senses, and on the senses alone (even in vocal music there exists "a charm anterior to expression"), whereas the mind becomes involved in the sensual pleasures. In sounds that have no definite meaning, "[the mind] seeks to establish relations or analogies with different objects, and with various impressions produced by nature . . . the slightest analogies, the weakest relations suffice." Morellet noted that, if one compares pieces where the great masters have sought to depict the same physical object, "one always, or almost always, finds something in common, whether in the movement, the rhythm, the intervals or the mode." And Chabanon added examples: a weak, continuous oscillation of two notes to render the murmuring of a brook; a cascade of rising or falling notes to express a clap of thunder, flash of lightning, or gust of wind; numerous basses playing in unison and rolling the melody for the sea; and so on.

A more comprehensive analysis, encompassing all known works in which the composer proposed to evoke some natural or moral phenomenon, would be required to discover underlying common structures. And like Morellet and Chabanon, I have no doubt that one would arrive at a number of invariants.

(In the second act of *Der Rosenkavalier,* and in the last bars of Debussy's *Pelléas et Mélisande*, the listener can perceive an analogy between the motifs formed by the slowly falling dissonant chords. But what is common to Arkel's desperate reflection on the human condition after Mélisande's death and love at first sight? It is because the love between Octavian and Sophie appears hopeless that it too must be expressed in the terms of a painful melancholy, as rendered by the orchestral twinges of sorrow—an expression that, for me, connotes the common denominator between the two situations, which the music renders almost physically.)

Chabanon (who had an interest in spiders and played the violin for them to see what kind of music they liked) took a further step, proposing a marvelous image that gives the idea of correspondence its full resonance. The philosophy of art, he claimed, has as its highest vocation to inform each sense taken separately of the contribution of the other senses to its experience. "In this manner the spider, sitting at the center of his web, corresponds with all its threads, living, as it were, in each of them; and (if, like our senses, the threads were animate) the spider would be able to transmit to each of the threads the perception given to it by all the others." (The spider was then in fashion: the same image of the spider's web as an extension of consciousness can be found in *Le Rêve de d'Alembert*,* which was written in 1769, but only appeared in 1831, long after Chabanon's death.)

These Baudelairean correspondences do not proceed primarily from the senses. Their effect on the senses depends on an intellectual operation (one misconceived by Diderot in his theory of hieroglyphics). "It is not, strictly speaking, for the ears that one draws visually striking musical pictures, but for the mind which, placed between the two senses, compares and combines their sensations," and grasps the invariant relations between them. There is no need to provide these relations with a content; they are forms. "The descending notes of a diatonic scale no more depict the descent of winter weather than any other descent." Should a musician wish to

---

*D'Alembert's Dream, by Diderot.

evoke the dawn, he need not portray "night and day, but just a contrast, any contrast. And the same music will express equally well any contrast one might imagine as that between light and shadow." The terms have no meaning in themselves; their relations alone matter.

15

It is something of a double paradox. The principles on which Saussure was to base his structural linguistics were clearly set forth during the middle of the eighteenth century in France, but in relation to music, by an author whose ideas were comparable to those we associate today with phonology—even though he held that, as a mode of expression, music is completely foreign to articulate speech.

Music is made up of sounds. "A musical sound by itself does not carry any signification. . . . Each sound is more or less empty, and has neither its own meaning nor character." In this regard, sounds differ from the elements of speech; words, syllables, and even letters can be characterized as long, short, fluid, and so forth, whereas "C and D on the scale do not have any differential properties." Relative to each "intrinsically empty" sound, music's appeal depends on the sounds that come before and after it.

As can be seen, Chabanon's ideas on music are quite advanced when compared to his ideas on language, which do not extend beyond the phonetic level. It was in reflections on music rather than language that the contours of modern linguistics took shape. In this sense, one could say that in the history of ideas "sonology" anticipated and prefigured phonology.

This temporal discrepancy is not unrelated to the absence in music of a level of articulation corresponding to vocabulary. Chabanon was fully aware of this absence. If music is a language, "this language has its characteristic elements, sounds; and it has phrases, which have a beginning, middle and end." Between the sounds and the phrases, however, there is nothing. Should nature have so desired, it could have made music serve our needs as articulate speech does: "For music to express and transmit ideas, convention has to associate the one with the other. And nothing could be easier." An accord of two notes three degrees apart could be made to signify "bread." But music has no dictionary. From this it follows that, if spoken language can express the same idea with different words, or with a different word order, such expression is impossible in music. "A word or turn of phrase is just the conventional sign of a thing; as it has synonyms or equivalencies, it can be replaced." In music, by contrast, "sounds are not the expression of a thing, but the thing itself."

One can also bring out Chabanon's modernity by comparing his ideas with those of two of the more important theorists of his time, Rousseau and Rameau. Unlike Rousseau, he did not tie the origin of music to that of articulate speech. Language cannot be derived, given the arbitrariness of the linguistic sign, from the imitation of objects or natural impressions; as such, there is nothing primitive in language. The origin of language is problematic, unlike that of singing, which emerged prior to and independently of language. "Instrumental music necessarily precedes vocal music; for when the voice sings without words, it is no more than an instrument." If one tries to relate the characteristics of singing to those of language, one will create a gulf between vocal and instrumental music. But every truly beautiful instrumental piece of music can be appropriated, with the aid of words, by the voice. "Bring us a thunderous symphony, and we will turn it into a choir, or even a dance." Chabanon, in effect, anticipated Beethoven's *Ninth Symphony* and Isadora Duncan.

In the eighteenth century, a great deal of audacity was required to affirm that a beautiful song could be appreciated without understanding the words, let alone that it could be better appreciated outside the stage. According to Chabanon, the sole advantage of music accompanied by words was that it helped those with feeble intelligence and little or no taste: "Purely instrumental music leaves their minds in suspense, uncertain as to its signification. . . . The more trained and sensitive one's ear . . . the easier it is to do without words, even when the voice is singing." And the preceding reservation notwithstanding, the same can even be said of the stage. Rameau, the "operatic symphonist," did not need words, for it was not the subject matter that inspired or generated his musical ideas: "No-one knows where he gets them from . . . once he has come up with a motif, he must continue. . . . This first idea generates several others." The celebrated modulation and accompaniment of Télaïre's aria in *Castor et Pollux* have inspired me with similar thoughts (*supra,* chapter 9).

In his conviction that words do not have any bearing on music, Chabanon ran counter to Rousseau, who denied the French language all musical qualities and concluded that Italian was superior because it was favored by a harmonious language. Chabanon refuted both Rousseau's argument and its elaboration by Sherlock, whose surname alone he gives (the author is in fact Martin Sherlock, and the book, *Nouvelles Lettres d'un voyageur anglais*, London and Paris, 1780, letter XXVI, p. 162—though it is not certain that the work is his). Chabanon not only considered French a musical language, thanks to the laxness of its pronunciation, its silent syllables (which songsters are able to turn to their advantage), and the facility with which the length of its syllables can be varied at will. He claimed that, in its relation to language, music is sovereign: "Music can render any language musical by bending it to its needs."

In opposition to Batteux, even more than to Rousseau, Chabanon considered the idea of a hierarchy of languages indefensible, whatever the criteria used (notably that of the language's "genius," so dear to Batteux). Again Chabanon is very much our contemporary. "All idioms establish, for those who speak and understand them correctly, an equally clear, concise and smooth communication of ideas. . . . All proper ideas rightfully belong to every idiom, and everyone has the means for their expression." Similarly, as regards their musical qualities: "No-one can . . . assign speech its euphonic qualities on the basis of constant, universal principles. Each language has its own principles." From which it follows that

> differences in taste and judgment, can only be explained, it seems to me, by the conventions established for different idioms. These conventions form so many prejudices, and these prejudices influence our sensations, modifying them without our awareness. Biased judgments deceive our senses.

Chabanon's feelings toward Rameau were mixed. They seem to have been on good terms, but if Chabanon delivered Rameau's funeral eulogy, he expressed the same reservations there as in his article "Sur la musique de l'Opéra de Castor" and his books. In fact, he kept his distance from both Rameau and Rousseau: from Rousseau, in that he gave precedence to instrumental over vocal music; and from Rameau, in that he affirmed the primacy of melody over harmony. The ear derives little pleasure from chords without a tune, but it can still find satisfaction in a tune without chords. Every gratifying musical composition, even an instrumental one, has a melody; one should not, therefore, oppose melody to composition. Rousseau condemned "conventional beauty, which has almost no other merit than the difficulty overcome; instead of good music, they [his adversaries] would have scholarly music . . . fugues, imitations and double subjects." To which Chabanon replied, rallying to Rameau's camp:

> What does one commonly mean by the words "scholarly music," which are on everyone's lips? . . . They serve to condemn music that one does not like (or does not want to like), and as if to console the Composer . . . leave him with the dubious compensation of a meaningless compliment.

Chabanon recognized that with Rameau music had taken an immense step forward, but that it would take a new turn after him. The "stream" of Lully's music had divided into two branches: the one, represented by Rameau, was "deep, vast, and wide-ranging" (Rousseau, by contrast, would have had music return to the point where Lully had left it); the other branch, "augmented by foreign waters, will be the music that we will have from now on." Ten years before Gluck went to Paris, this judgment would prove prophetic.

What Chabanon admired in Rameau bore little relation to the latter's self-proclaimed ambitions. Rameau's greatness lay in his melodic imagination: "What made him a man of genius was the completely original character of his tunes and their prodigious variety. Rameau was a creator of melodies. As regards harmony, he was simply, and could scarcely have been more than, a profound theorist." But undue importance should not be attributed to this latter role. His harmonic embellishments were often "limited, commonplace and trite," and generally reducible to "vivid impressions within everyone's reach." Above all, harmony does not have firm, definitive laws. Even Rameau, who believed in such laws and claimed to have discovered them, immediately had to add that "the exceptions are almost as frequent as the rule."

Art, according to Chabanon, never proceeds from theoretical reflection; it precedes the latter and provides it with its subject matter: "A bold, fortuitous stroke by the artist who creates spontaneously, becomes a new revelation for the theorist who reasons." This from the *Éloge de M. Rameau.* . . . In *De la musique,* Chabanon insisted that the creator is not conscious of the laws he discovers. "The philosophical mind, when applied to the Fine Arts, can play but a secondary role." The arts have their logic, but "this logic differs so much from that of the calm tranquil mind, that the latter cannot be employed to fathom the former."

Once harmony has been dislodged from the pedestal on which Rameau had placed it, its relation to melody can be better understood. The one is, to put it briefly, a function of the other: "Every tune suggests a bass harmony, and every chord progression can be the basis of a thousand concordant tunes." This rule admits no exception, not even among the Africans or the American savages, whose music contains "harmonic parts unsuspected by their inventors." But in what sense, then, do melody and harmony differ? Melody is defined as a continuous sequence of sounds that allows but one arrangement, whereas harmony is the storehouse and repertory of sounds that melody can employ. "[Harmony] is the mine from which melody draws its sounds, and whose labor force it [melody] employs." This distinction corresponds to that made by modern linguists between the syntagmatic chain and the paradigmatic sets. When Chabanon, by way of summary, wrote that "melody implies succession, and harmony, simultaneity," he anticipated the very terms of the Saussurean relation, fundamental to the analysis of language, between the "axis of successions" and the "axis of simultaneities."

16

In his reflections on music, Chabanon discovered the same properties that structural linguistics would attribute to language. Yet Chabanon did not perceive the two domains as analogous. In his most important work, when turning from music to language, he announced that he would not limit his thinking to what they might have in common. This is an understatement, for he went to considerable effort to stress their differences, principally that "in music the intervals can be discerned by the ear and measured, while in speech they are neither discernible nor measurable."

Structural linguistics would overcome this difficulty by demonstrating that, from a formal perspective, the phoneme, constituted from distinctive features, and the musical chord are analogous. Chabanon, moreover, did appear to have a vague awareness that language too has a structure.

If our taste for analogy (which is synonymous with our propensity for imitation), if such an aptitude were not instinctual, all language would be but a confused jumble of words and expressions which allows of neither principle, order, or connection. And if this were the case, even the most capacious memory would hardly be sufficient to possess a language.

That the mind does indeed possess languages is due to its grasp of the invariant relations in language structure. Diderot, in his attempt to resolve the problem of time's unity in painting, arrived at this same idea, if somewhat confusedly (*supra*, chapter 11).

In the third chapter of the second part of his book, *Considérations sur les langues* (in which one can read, by way of opposition, Rousseau's *Essai sur l'origine des langues**), Chabanon demonstrated the consistency of his thought by rejecting the idea that the evolution of languages can be explained by external influences, especially climate. The latter has not changed in Greece, or in Rome "whose genius bore its gifts to the Gauls, Picts and Germans, even as the Romans believed that these peoples were destined to remain barbarians by the nature of the places they inhabited." Far from being pliable as a result of climate, the speech organ is the least flexible of organs. In order to spare itself the effort, it seeks the easiest, gentlest articulation—thus the conversion of the *r* into *l*. The favorable climate enjoyed by the Marseillais has not prevented their pronunciation from being harsh and guttural. And Russian is one of the mellowest languages in Europe, despite the rough climate, and so on.

All this was to be a rigorous refutation of Rousseau and, more generally, naturalism—that stain on much of the philosophical thought of the eighteenth century. In truth, Chabanon's ideas on articulate speech and the problems it poses were much sounder

---

Essay on the Origin of Lanuages.

than those of his contemporaries, beginning with Rousseau. Since all languages possess the same capacities, one cannot attribute to each a particular genius (here Chabanon was thinking of Batteux). The specificity of a given language is related to the historical circumstances of its employment. Once men of learning begin to write, "thought sets to work: ideas are put into motion and wander amongst all the materials of language, turning the whole storehouse upside down to find the appropriate words." Alternatively, they might associate a word, by virtue of some distant analogy, with some other idea and thereby give it a new meaning. As the products of the human mind become more sophisticated, its use of language becomes more subtle. But this does not mean that the language itself has improved. Chabanon was by no means convinced that Malherbe and Guez de Balzac had discovered "the true genius of our language"; on the contrary, he looked back nostalgically at the language of Ronsard, Amyot, and Montaigne. It is quite permissible to criticize Ronsard's artistic theories, but not his language. One must be careful not to ascribe a work's faults or merits to the language in which it is written.

If the search for concordance in language presupposes the operations of the intellect, the opposite is the case in music. In music one seeks first to please the ear; the impressions that aim to satisfy the mind come after. Chabanon believed this opposition to be deeply rooted.

In his view, language has two contradictory aspects. Everyone is endowed with speech; it is a natural and universal faculty. But at the same time, languages are necessarily conventional, given both their diversity and the arbitrariness of the linguistic sign, which renders the different language groups mutually unintelligible.

Music, on the other hand, since it is without words and cannot signify, falls entirely within the province of the sensations. It is a universal language whose principles proceed from humans' physical makeup (and that of animals as well—Chabanon was convinced, from his experiments on the violin, that spiders and "certain small fish living in the mud" appreciate music). As music is built on the real, natural relations between sounds, there is, and there can be, nothing conventional about it. With only minor differences, melody everywhere has necessarily the same basis. And the proof is that, though no one understands all languages, everyone responds to music, whatever its origin. Europeans, for example, are responsive to music from Asia, and even from Africa or America.

Chabanon's major source as regards America seems to have been a certain M. Marin, a French officer who, it was said, had lived among the natives. M. Marin would sing what he remembered of their tunes, while Chabanon sought to reproduce them on his violin by playing different variations until Marin recognized—or thought he recognized—what he had first heard in America. A number of years ago Mme. Betsy Jolas tried, in a similar manner, to play on the piano all the possible ways of rendering my rather amateurish notations of the music of the Nambikwara and Tupi-Kawahib. I kept those transcriptions that evoked a more accurate echo in my memory (these were to be published in a collective work, but the editor of the volume lost them in a taxi—and to this day I still begrudge his memory). I, at least, was aware of the weaknesses of this procedure (though, unlike Marin, I was not singing what I thought I could remember, but had noted the tunes down on the spot). Chabanon, however, does not appear to have doubted his informant, who provided him with Indian songs denatured by a European ear, as evidenced by the transcriptions. Rousseau was more perceptive, and said that, although the transcriptions of exotic music may "cause some to admire the soundness and universality of our rules, they may lead others to question the intelligence or fidelity of those who transmitted these tunes to us."

Though Chabanon admitted the equivalent distinction for language, he did not distinguish between music understood as natural and universal (all peoples have music) and musics, which—contrary to what he claims—differ as much among themselves as do languages. He viewed sounds as agreeable sensations like colors or smells. But the analogy does not hold, for if nature encompasses colors and smells, its reach does not extend to musical sounds, only to noises. The art of sounds lies entirely within the domain of culture. (Chabanon, by contrast, remained true to his ideas, claiming that music was a language so natural to man that "in this regard it should not even be called an Art.") The tendency to present gratuitous affirmations as experiential givens was a vice common to eighteenth-century philosophical thought. Chabanon was not exempt from this tendency, as when he declared that the birds do not sing in order to communicate with each other, but simply to express their joy at the fine weather.

In *The Raw and the Cooked* I discussed the argument concerning bird song. In order not to leave the eighteenth century, I will limit myself here to Marmontel's position as presented in his article "Liberal Arts" in the *Encylopédie*. The idea that music, as the art of arranging and combining sounds into a system of modulations and chords, could be related to bird song or the accents of the human voice was in his view ridiculous:

Each of the senses has its purely physical pleasures, like taste and smell. The ear especially has its own gratifications, and seems to be all the more sensitive to the latter as they are rarer in nature. For the thousand agreeable sensations accorded the sense of sight, the sense of hearing receives perhaps not even one. . . . Everything in the universe appears made for the eyes, and almost nothing for the ears. Thus, of all the arts, the one best suited to rival nature, is the art of melody and harmony.

It would appear that Marmontel was here refuting Chabanon's claims word for word. But his article appeared in 1776, in volume I of the *Supplément* to the *Encyclopédie,* and he could not, therefore, have known about even the first version of Chabanon's work. Nor was I able to find any mention of Chabanon's name in Marmontel's *Mémoires.* Morellet's name, however, appears often, for they were old friends (late in his life, Marmontel married Morellet's young niece and lived with his in-laws under the same roof). It is therefore tempting to see this article as reflecting the differences of opinion, and even the heated diferences (as recalled by Marmontel in his *Mémoires*), which often brought them into conflict, despite their mutual affection and respect.

Chabanon was too intelligent not to sense the weaknesses of a purely naturalist conception of music. In his *Éloge de M. Rameau* he tempered this conception, admitting that music, though a universal language, is still differentiated into dialects. But how far do these differences extend? In his most important work, he considered the possible correlations between music and what we today would call national character.

> To verify that each Nation is endowed by Nature with its own characteristic music . . . would be to add a Chapter, or at least a paragraph, to man's history. What would be the result if one were to follow through on this discovery, and clearly establish connections between the music of each nation and its character, morals, language, and its particularities relative to all the Arts?

One goes from one extreme to the other. Such oscillation by Chabanon is demonstrated by another passage. If the Chinese or

Africans have a different sense of physical beauty, when transported to Europe they adopt our own views: "The homage paid by these exotic foreigners to our sense of beauty proves that it is universal, [unless] the Africans and Chinese have simply changed prejudices." As soon as the existence of universal values is placed in doubt, cultural relativism raises its head. And Chabanon was not satisfied with extending this relativism to music (at least as a hypothesis), but went so far as to conceive that for any given people analogous relations might exist between its music and its painting, poetry, and language. But the idea was quickly rejected as too many objections came to mind.

According to Chabanon, within societies the arts do not all develop at the same pace. In the century of Louis XIV, poetry, painting, and eloquence all shone brilliantly, while music scarcely left the shadows. This time lag is all the more remarkable given that "although Music only advances after the other Arts, it precedes them in its origin." Such matters can only be clarified by an ethnographic inquiry. The person who undertook such a difficult task would certainly present new and interesting facts for philosophical contemplation, but it is imperative that that person make a musical voyage around the world. The music of the black people on the Gold Coast is sad and plodding, the music of Angola is light and lively, and that of America's native peoples, calm and tranquil. Spanish dances are solemn and majestic; Polish dancing has a more pronounced rhythm and tends toward haughtiness. English dancing is characterized by rapid movements, German dancing is spirited and fiery, while French dances are cheerful, gracious, and dignified. Italy, however, does not have any dances [*sic*].

Now travelers claim that the Africans of the Gold Coast also differ from those of Angola in terms of their temperament and morals. "Can one not multiply such examples? [With music] Nature would then have endowed the peoples of the world with a language that reveals their innermost character." There are cases, however, in which the music and the behavior do not accord, for example, the gentle, graceful singing that accompanies the cannibal feasts of the American Indians. If the analogy between music and morals can be verified for Spain, it cannot for England. How much faith can one put in this analogy? Perhaps certain superficial traits are analogous, but not the deeper ones?

At any rate, the analogy does not hold for Europe, where enlightenment, intellect, taste, and the fine arts circulate among peoples. Discoveries, principles, and methods have flowed in successive waves from one end of the continent to the other. The free exchange of the arts has caused them to lose their *indigenous* character (Chabanon's emphasis). This is particularly true for music, apart from a few differences at the level of performance. And should one claim that these latter differences reflect national character, one would have to find for each nation comparable differences in the other arts.

With these considerations the distinction, which Chabanon deemed fundamental, between music and articulate speech returns to the foreground, but the perspectives opened up are rather different from those that he had first discerned. Eloquence, poetry, and theater have, in his view, an immediate and necessary relation to the character, customs, morals, and government of each nation. As these arts are "the mind's offspring and enliven speech," they are narrowly dependent on local, historical circumstances. Music depicts neither persons nor things and as such does not have the same dependency: thus one hears the same music in Rome, London, and Madrid. But then how does one explain the internal contradictions? The Germans, though "harsh and prickly melodicists are such sweet, genial and sensitive Poets. . . . And the Italian who sang in the French manner eighty years ago, did he really possess our Nation's morals?"

The universality of music proclaimed at the beginning of the work is based on the sensory organization common to all humans and even animals. Later, when restricted to Europe, this universality is explained in terms of a set of historical, cultural, and social conditions. But even here it cannot be claimed that musical taste, once dissociated from sense impressions, reveals the national spirit to be concordant: for, within a given people, the arts sometimes clash with the national temperament. "I fear" admits Chabanon, "that the most enlightened philosophy scarcely throws any light on these mysteries."

If this is the case, one has to conclude that, on the one hand, "the character of a nation's most popular songs does not provide a sure guide to its character or genius"; on the other, "the difference between the speech arts, which are judged primarily by the mind, and the art of sounds, which has to appeal to the tribunal of the ear, is so great that a dull people may still be good musicians, while a people with deep thoughts have only light music." Nonetheless, the difference between music and speech is not as great as one might think, since between the two lies the recitative.

The problem of the recitative obsessed Chabanon, and a mind as profound as his could not fail to perceive its philosophical implications. "A sort of amphibious monster, half song, half declamation," the recitative is the principal defect of opera, especially French opera. Rameau's major failing was that he did not know how to overcome this obstacle. This is not a problem in concerts, where there is just music, but it becomes problematic when the theatrical moment is preponderant as a result of situational interest. How is music to render dramatic action? No one knows. In these matters, the theory remains uncertain and advice is almost impossible to give.

All one can do is note, as a matter of experience, the existence of "a secret affinity between the inflections of speech and the sentiments that determine them." One cannot explain this affinity; it constitutes "an impenetrable, metaphysical mystery." Different peoples have different intonations, and sometimes those of one people are the inverse of those of another. Hence the two contrary observations: "The principles of intonation were not instituted by Nature. But they are not conventional either. Their causation is unknown, like that of the various accents in different countries."

Opera, it is believed, can get out of this predicament by way of the recitative, "singing diminished . . . by the loss of its rhythmic precision . . . a step towards simple speech." But even with a superior recitative, if one doesn't know the words, one will never guess their meaning. "The recitative's modes of expression appear extremely limited; the same modes are often repeated." It is necessary to refer to the words. But nonetheless ties are woven between the words and the music: "The meaning of the words throws a different light on the sounds."

The gap separating music and language is not, therefore, quite as large as one thought: there is a conventional moment in music, and there is a natural moment in speech. Thus the need, in opera, for an intimate collaboration between the musician and the poet. They may both hear and speak only their own language, but they must both know how to render each of their arts complementary to the other. Hence the rather curious claim "Opera desires a double birth."

In the "Réflexions préliminaires" that opens *De la Musique,* Chabanon announced that he would consider the art of music "in terms of its skeletal anatomy." What he was proposing to discover, he claimed, is the underlying nature or basic idea behind all the other ancillary ideas. And once he discovered that melody is the most elementary idea of music conceivable, he had only to extrapolate from the idea to reconstitute music in its entirety.

He thus came to see music as a language common to all times and all peoples. No doubt this is true for the skeleton. Musical language has its own structure—a structure that both brings it near to articulate speech (sounds, like phonemes, do not have any intrinsic meaning) and distances it from that same speech (the language of music does not have a level of articulation corresponding to words). Up to this point, Chabanon's argument remains quite plausible.

However, it does not follow from the universality of this structure that the content of musical language is always the same, with only minor variations. Once Chabanon deepened his analysis, he was forced to retreat. If at first the theory encompassed all music, it gradually contracted to the consideration of Western music alone. The latter, beginning in the eighteenth century, had become detached from music in general and formed its own separate universe. Chabanon was to pay increasing attention to this phenomenon, having recognized that it suggested a most singular history: "With the first few steps [French music] took to distance itself from the simple popular songs (like the old Christmas carols), it was diverted from its true path." One still knows what, at a formal level, distinguishes music from speech, but the idea that music, in contrast to language, would be largely the same throughout the world—this idea lapses into a nothingness from which Chabanon should never have sought to retrieve it.

18

While I was reading the second part of Chabanon's work *De la Musique*, largely devoted to opera, Michel Leiris's *Operratiques,* a posthumous collection of fragments that he had wanted to publish under this title, appeared. Beyond the observations of a more ethnological character on Chinese theater, voodoo rites, and the Greek Karagheuz, these notes contain many other penetrating reflections: for example, on verism, "a naturalism that retains only certain paroxystic elements from reality"; on Monteverdi's expressionism, Puccini's lyricism, and the Wagnerism of *Pelléas* (where, it would appear, he has taken up a number of observations that I often heard expressed by our mutual friend, René Leibowitz); or his comments on *Parsifal* ("If a theatrical performance is, as Wagner conceived, a rite, then one should avoid, precisely, staging the simulacrum of a rite") and the critique of Menotti.

Then there are judgments whose simplicity is disconcerting. Leiris credits Puccini's *Tosca* with the themes of oppression and torture because of their renewed relevance. And he reproaches Wagner's *Die Meistersinger* for its "disagreeable chauvinism," on the pretext that it has Hans Sachs defend the spirit of German music against all foreign influences (but Wagner's use of the adjective *wälsch,** when placed in the mouth of an ardent reformer, applies to all Roman and Catholic peoples; and one knows how much music owes to Luther, and later to Wagner himself: he, of all people, has the right to make the transposition).

Other judgments are frankly shocking. For someone who understands Puccini so well, Leiris is not afraid to make Leoncavallo his equal. And why? Leoncavallo, he claims, demonstrated his genius "by bringing together within a single work the following two themes—the tears beneath the laughter, and the truth beneath the staged appearance." The words *brilliant* and *genius* appear three times in two pages in the discussion of the libretto of *I Pagliacci*. But regarding the music, not a word.

It is quite surprising that, in a work that is often spellbinding, and where some fifty operas are the object of commentaries full of grace and poetry, there is almost never any discussion of the music.

In his *Journal,* published a few months after *Operratiques,* Leiris relates his impressions of a performance of *Parsifal* he attended in 1954. Again there is the comment cited earlier, as well as two additional pages of criticisms. Now I too do not relish breathing in the stale odor of religiosity that on occasion pervades *Parsifal.* But Christian travesties of the Grail cycle are not of recent date: they go back to the beginning of the thirteenth century and Robert de Boron. For the ethnologist, who owes it to himself to become familiar with religious history, this tradition is eminently respectable. Instead of becoming irritated, it would have been better

---

*"Foreigner," more especially, the speakers of Romance languages.

had he tried to understand this tradition and situate the innovations of the Wagnerian version in relation to the other successive versions since Chrétien de Troyes. But beyond all else, on reading these pages, it does not appear that during the course of the performance Leiris had any feeling for the music. For my part, when I hear the music of *Parsifal* I find myself overcome, and all questioning ceases.

Leiris's interest is limited to the vocal merits and acting abilities of the singers, and to the staging, the decor, and, above all else, the dramatic action. No writer on opera has ever given so much importance to anecdote (there is something of Diderot in Leiris). Whatever the story, if one will allow me the expression, "it works."

It may work, but I have trouble following. With the exception of only a few librettos—those of the Ring cycle (for reasons I have developed elsewhere); that of *Carmen* and, even more, *Die Meistersinger*, a masterpiece about the birth of the masterpiece (Leiris admits to "turning up his nose at it in distaste"); that of *Pelléas* (another opera that inspires in Leiris a certain reticence), which, contrary to present opinion, I find admirable—most leave me indifferent. There are few operas in which I feel the need to understand the words; once I have learned the story, I immediately forget it. When I hear *Lucia di Lammermoor* anew on the radio, recalling the plot would, I believe, add nothing to the emotion produced by the fortissimo of the sextuor, that thrill I experience listening to the aria of madness when beautifully sung.

But what then, for me, is opera? It is a great adventure. I embark on a ship whose rigging, with its masts, sails, and ropes, brings together all the instrumental and vocal means the composer requires to complete the voyage. I hear compressed into three or four hours a prodigious amount of music: music that is as varied as the spectacle of the world and yet still holds together (didn't Chabanon stress that opera "can admit several styles within the same work . . . belonging to different musical periods"?); music that transports me to a world of sounds a thousand miles from all terrestrial concerns, as though I had suddenly found myself in the middle of the ocean.

Consequently I no longer go to the opera. I have a sense of foreboding that the vessel will sink beneath the intolerable weight of the staging and decor, which insult both the music and the poetry. The only questions that the producer need ask (though here the conductor suffices, for he at least knows and respects the work) are, What did the composer see in his head, and how can he best reconstitute it armed with the technical means presently available (but, please, no cinematographic projections mixed in with the decor; opera demands the stylization of reality)? In 1876 Wagner was said to have been unhappy with the staging of the Ring cycle, because it had not lived up to his imagination (while a child, I saw the *Ride of the Valkyries* represented by the singers rolling in little chariots of the Roman type over a series of inclines—something that made a lot of noise). Contrary to what one might believe, or want to believe, Wagner had very definite ideas about the scenography and expected them to be realized. He wrote to the producer of *Lohengrin:*

> You have changed the decor a bit, for example, the course of the river in the first act. . . . I would have liked, in the castle courtyard, the balcony and stairway leading from the Kemenate to the Palas to be more in view . . . by moving the tower of the Palas back a little to the right.

And relative to a production of *Tannhäuser* that he had not attended: "I have been told that the *Sängerhalle* was a great success in Berlin; however, I do not believe that it conformed to my stage directions (for I cannot consent to abandoning the open air arcade with the stairway and courtyard)."

Treating such instructions lightly strikes me as being just as serious a matter as handling the text or music infelicitously. I would go so far as to wish that, in the theater as well, the older works would always be represented as intended and conceived by their authors. "Everyone is aware," wrote Hannetaire, an eighteenth-century author and actor, "of the success with which Mlle. Champmêlé played, amongst her other roles, that of Phédre, which Racine had shown to her Verse by Verse, and whose recitation, it is said, could have been written down and transmitted, if only one had the necessary characters." Left to the devices of actors and stage managers, classical declamation and decoration have, unfortunately, been lost. If the stylistic splendor of the costumes and rules of diction had been codified by a theoretician like Zeami, we would not marvel so much at the nô theater.

Stage managers, whether because they lack culture or because they have been fed a diet of false ideas, drag the Wagnerian gods and heroes down to the stage floor and mobilize them in the service of the ideologies of the moment. It is a crude misinterpretation. Wagner began by writing historical operas but did not continue, for he became convinced that myth alone is true for all time, and that the truth of history lies with myth, and not the converse.

My admiration for the prose writer and poet notwithstanding, I feel rather distant from Leiris, with his toleration for such distortions, and closer to Chabanon, who had healthier notions concerning opera. Wasn't he the one who praised Rameau as a symphonist, whose ideas did not need words for their expression, even in opera?

In Chabanon's eyes, opera raises two issues. First, though the genre appears absurd in its principle, it is a success in practice. And second, if opera has progressed (to the point where, he claimed, the works of previous centuries are no longer worth seeing) it is not because of the lyrics, as La Bruyère had hoped, or the spectacle, which still remains at a draft stage: it is the music alone that has improved.

Concerning the first point, Chabanon stressed that, despite appearances, music is fully compatible with tragedy, and its attempt to inspire terror and pity by words and acts. Singing accompanies speech and action in everyday life—women sing as they spin and sew, as does the artisan as he works, and so forth. Music is also present during such terrible tragedies as funerals or wars. What appears so "monstrously absurd" about opera is the fact that those who are singing are precisely those doing the killing, dying, and grieving.

This, however, merely exemplifies that higher order of implausibility that always exists in the theater, "a magical enclosure wherein time and space are contracted"—the very idea Wagner will, in *Parsifal,* place in the mouth of Gurnemanz to give the scene of the transformation its transcendent significance. Now "anything implausible that produces an imposing effect, bears within itself . . . its own legitimacy and eminence. . . . The music is an additional marvel, which renders the others all the more convincing." Music heightens the spectacle's majesty, for it can compensate for the silence of the person meditating by arousing the audience's awareness, through symphonic means, of the presence of a violent passion (in which case, the principal theme is borne by the orchestra). Or it can replace "the idle chatter of confidants" with a choir that acts as "the interpreter of the emotions transmitted by a group in a state of excitation to a throng of listeners."

As for the second issue—that the music alone improves, and not the verse—it can be explained by the fact that, in order for opera to progress, the music and poetry must evolve in opposite directions. This was the merit of Lully's librettist, Quinault, who innovated by placing "tragedy under music's apprenticeship." He sought to avoid making matters complicated by searching for "the marvelous in his subject matter, and simplicity in his manner of treating it."

Similarly Leiris will say that opera is redeemed by "an excess of convention." And he approves of Hoffman's having asked the librettist to ensure that "the spectators, though they barely understand a word of the text, can still get an idea of the plot from what they see happening" (but, further on, Leiris admits that he would not have listened to the choruses of *Mahogany* with such emotion, had he not understood the words). As an amusing aside, one might note that Leiris levels the same reproach at Wagner's "very long and complicated" poetry as Chabanon directed at Voltaire's librettos: in both cases the music demands retrenchment, for "in lyrical genres, it all comes down to simplicity."

> Wherever lyric Tragedy has been established, it first adopts simple mythological subjects. . . . The poetic universe created by the imagination of the Ancients, teeming with invention and aglitter with spirited fantasies' appears as if prepared beforehand for Music's enchantment.

Though I was not aware of this passage when writing *The Naked Man,* I would now add it in support of the thesis advanced in the "Finale," that the music of the seventeenth and eighteenth centuries adopted the structures of mythic thought for its own purposes.

There are, to be sure, operas with historical subject matter. Leiris wonders whether "historical opera . . . responds to that period when the bourgeoisie was making, preparing to make, or had just made . . . its revolution against tyranny?" Chabanon settles this matter in a rather abrupt manner. The music based on the poetry of Metastasio, which replaces fable with history, is simply boring, and that is why "no-one listens to opera in Italy."

Chabanon, however, feared shocking his contemporaries by appearing to limit opera to the marvelous. He could have drawn support from Batteux, who, writing in 1746, believed that in opera's spectacle, "the Gods [should] act as gods, with all the instruments of their supernatural power. What is not marvelous ceases, in a sense, to be plausible. . . . An opera can thus be defined as the representation of a marvelous idea." (La Bruyère had already criticized Lully for having caused the stage machinery to vanish. And Chabanon leveled a not unrelated critique, when he accused Lully of having introduced madrigals and insipid ditties into the opera.) Objects of wonder speak to the eyes, as the passions to the soul. Opera unites wonder and passion with the addition of a third enchantment, music. It is a form of theater in which, as Leiris says, "spectacle, music and pure drama converge on the spectator's emotions . . . and entirely besiege him."

The evolution that led to the development of opera therefore accords with the logic of things:

> In France Corneille and Racine had taken tragedy, so to speak, to its highest point, when Music sought to combine it with vocalized sounds. . . . The century that admired *Phèdre* and the *Horaces* could not condemn this innovation, but sought instead to become equally enthusiastic about *Armide*.

I perceive a certain similarity, expressed in almost the same terms, between Chabanon's conception of the passage from spoken to lyric tragedy and my own attempt to establish a continuity between myth and music: "It is," he writes, "when Tragedy, in its perfection, appears to have exhausted all its possibilities and cannot but enter into decline, that Music undertakes to reproduce Tragedy in a new form." Thus France's literary history would illustrate, on a rather reduced scale, a development that I believe to be typical of Western civilization as a whole. But why did Chabanon add, "At least this undertaking is consolation for our decadence"?

In truth, he was highly distrustful of fashion or "mannerisms" and warned against modernism's vertigo.

> When our disdainful forgetfulness condemns musical productions that are only twenty years old to oblivion, you can mark the date when your own productions will be similarly condemned. What is one to make of this rapid succession of death notices, by means of which art, after having been destroyed piece-meal, will ultimately perish in its entirety?

If musical judgment can be accused of arbitrariness, and if the idea of the beautiful has come to be seen as purely conventional, the blame lies with the rapid revolutions that music undergoes every twenty or thirty years. "Let us not impoverish or exhaust Art by reducing it to its most modern productions." Chabanon is particularly impressed by the greatness of art's beginnings. "The simple beauties, which were discovered by art's pioneers, appear all the more true as their discovery was generally effortless; they have about them a sort of natural clarity."

Toward the beginning of his book Chabanon observed, when speaking of the droning music of sailors and peasants, that "they sing sadly with gaiety." In light opera, too, the music appears incapable of adapting itself to the humor of the situation. It always remains serious, even in works reputed to be comical or farcical. When in the service of comedy, music should depict the ridiculous and provoke laughter. But it cannot do so because (and the idea is profound) laughter bubbles up when it catches the intellect by surprise—and music has only an indirect relation to the intellect. Thus the most cheerful song does not trigger laughter, whereas a sentimental song causes the tears to flow. Can this obstacle be overcome? Chabanon dreamed of just such a possibility in a brilliant passage worth citing almost in its entirety.

> The musician who invents the art of which I am speaking . . . will have to instruct the actors to enact and articulate the recitative differently from the usual manner. But the orchestral flourishes that accompany his recitative, as well as the snatches of melody interspersed throughout, will have a humorous character indicative of the composer's intentions. Only with the aid of an entirely new talent and a strong sense of what is appropriate can one attempt to create what I am imagining. The Artist who would devote himself to such a project, will have to mold the Lyricist with whom he collaborates, the Actors who perform it, and perhaps the Public that listens to it. The education of the latter, though, will not be difficult.

Isn't this precisely the program that Mozart carried out, or was going to carry out, in *The Abduction from the Seraglio, Così* (Despina), and *The Magical Flute*? And then Rossini, and Offenbach, followed by Ravel, who, in *L'Heure espagnole,* raised the genre to its ultimate point of perfection?

I am not going to add *L'Enfant et les sortilèges* to this list, for each time I hear it, I find that I can't get over the fact that Ravel let himself be trapped by a libretto of unbearable intellectual and moral vulgarity (which, in this case, cannot be ignored by the listener, as it reins in the music and cuts it up into descriptive vignettes). In this libretto the author tastelessly stages her own apotheosis as a castrating mother ("*Songez, songez surtout au chagrin de maman*"*), along with a child, whom she calls "Baby" though he is of school age, and a host of servile animals at her feet.

In the two preludes, the ragtime, the scene with the princess, as well as the admirable final chorus, Ravel's genius rises to the surface. But scattered throughout are too many conventionalisms. In the face of the furniture trio, the cat duo, the entry of Arithmetic, and the scene of the injury, one cannot but deplore the composer's docility before the directives of the librettist.

---

*"Think about your mother's distress above all else."

Sounds and Colors

19

In the eighteenth century Father Louis-Bertrand Castel (1688–1757) was famous for the invention of an ocular or chromatic clavichord—which, one should add, he never managed to construct. Rousseau, Diderot, and Voltaire all mocked the idea that the play of colors could satisfy the sense of sight the way music satisfies that of hearing. On the other hand, a composer as important as Telemann took the idea seriously.

Contrary to the claims of his critics, Castel clearly understood that colors and sounds have a different nature: "It is of the essence of sound to be transient and fleeting; sound is tied immutably to time, and dependent on movement. . . . Color is subject to place, and is fixed and permanent. It stands out when standing still." Moreover, "while it is true that the acoustic opposition between low and high sounds is analogous to the visual opposition between dark and light, the latter exists independently of color (a scene can be represented in black and white), but the two differences are reunited in sound, it not being possible to produce low and high

Claude Lévi-Strauss

sounds that are not tones." In a sense, Castel anticipated the discovery by neurologists that optical stimuli, in their movement
from the retina to the cortex, follow one of three neural channels;
and that the luminance channel is distinct from the two color-
opponent channels (one for red and green, the other for yellow
and blue). Castel therefore had reason for thinking at the time,
"All this concern with colors is newer than one thinks." He himself, he went on to say, will have made "only a very small portion
of the immense discoveries that I foresee reserved for the centuries
to come, in spite of what the overly timid partisans of the incomparable Mr. Newton might say." In opposition to Newton, who
"thought that all the colors of the prism were primitive," Castel
would have been able to draw comfort from the findings of neu-
rology, which has taught us why the only pure colors humans perceive, aside from white and black, are red, green, yellow, and blue.

Castel, however, did not reason about colors as a neurobiolo-
gist or physicist. He posed the problem—and this was his great
originality—in ethnological terms, approaching it from the perspective of what we would today call material culture. His concern was with colors that are "substantial, ordinary and easy to
handle." His *Optics* "is to be a theory for Painters and Dyers." And
he was well aware that color appreciation varies among cultures.
In France, we prefer a golden yellow, "leaving the English to a
pure yellow, which we find bland." Castel may well have put his
finger on a cultural invariant: in an article dated June 10, 1992,
from *Le Figaro,* which describes a visit to France by Queen Elizabeth II, one reads that the sovereign was "dressed in a very
lemony yellow, which baffled more than one specialist."

With his detailed technical knowledge Castel arrived at a
rather surprising theory: "Black is composed of a profusion of colors. . . . There are good reasons for deriving color from black."
What good reasons? If white results from the mixture of all colors,

they are all latent in black; in a sense, it generates them. As proof Chabanon points to matter, which "by itself is dark and inanimate." When black iron is heated, it takes on all the different colors until it becomes white. Dyers, in order to obtain black, dip their fabric into each of the three primary colors in turn. Finally, if black is a dye, white is not, for it is denuded of the luxuriance that is black's inherent property. "Everything comes from black only to lose itself in white."

This is, to be sure, an extravagant doctrine, and not without its contradictions. Had not Diderot described Castel as "a black Brahman, half mad and half sane"? Still, he did have a sharp eye for colors, and a sensitivity to the effects of the material, the grain, and multiple dyes on coloring. And he was able, on the basis of his natural gifts and practical knowledge, to formulate a logic of sense impressions in which considerations of relation and opposition were in the foreground.

According to Castel, sounds and colors are no more identical, equal, or similar to each other than are lines and surfaces, or finite and infinite numbers in geometry. But between finite numbers the same properties exist as between infinite numbers, and the same properties exist between surfaces, bodies, or even properties, as between lines. The properties of sounds and colors are also, within their respective domains, analogous; "Everything is relative . . . an attractive relation extends its attractions to the two terms of the comparison. . . . Things stand out by virtue of their opposition." Castel (who was a mathematician) was to apply the theory of the fourth proportional to the fine arts, and in terms that would appear, were the idea not so old, to have been borrowed by the *Entretien entre d'Alembert et Diderot.**

---

*Diderot's "Conversation between D'Alembert and Diderot."

In seeking to revolutionize commonly held ideas about the color black, Castel created a precedent. In a sense, his theory, with its keen sensitivity to color, anticipates another attempt to overturn black's significance. I am thinking of what Rimbaud will essay in his sonnet *Voyelles** (which has been reproduced at the end of this chapter for the reader's convenience).

While speaking about "colored hearing" (a particular case of the correspondences between the senses designated by the term *synesthesia)*, Jakobson made the following comment: "The apparent connection between an optimally chromatic color such as scarlet and the optimally chromatic trumpet-ring and the summits of vocalic (/a/) and consonantal (/k/) chromaticity in the color name scarlet is indeed spectacular. . . . " (The original was written in English, but what is valid for "scarlet" is even more valid for the French *écarlate*.)

Numerous studies held in a variety of languages have demonstrated that the phoneme /a/ generally evokes the color red. (This is particularly true for children; colored hearing becomes rarer, or less clear, in most adults, though it can still be detected by indirect means). By way of an example, let me cite the wonderful anecdote reported by Clavière, one of the first authors to turn his attention to the phenomenon. An amateur boatsman once told him: "I am a sailor and . . . find the practice of placing a red light [*feu rouge*] on the starboard to be both natural and logical. . . . On the other hand, the word fire [*feu*] appears to me to be rather inappropriate, for fire is red, but the word has no *a* sound." That Rimbaud made the *a* sound black appears, therefore, as something of a

---

*"Vowels."

phonetic and visual scandal, imputable to that taste for provocation that the poet demonstrated on other occasions. But look again.

A, *noir corset velu de mouches éclatantes**

When discussing Manet's portrait of Berthe Morisot with a bunch of violets, Valéry will use this same adjective: "the black that belongs to Manet alone . . . the shiny [*éclatantes*] swatches of pure black . . . the full power of these blacks. . . . "

Eclatantes contains the phonemes /a/ and /k/, the "summits of vocalic and consonantal chromaticity." In a passage from Rimbaud's *Illuminations* about beauty, black is associated with the words *éclatent* and *écarlates* (the latter at the center of Jakobson's argument):

> *des blessures écarlates et noires éclatent*
> *dans les chairs superbes†*

The verses of the sonnet dedicated to the vowel *a* speak of the color black. Nonetheless, in the phonetism of *éclatantes*, red exists in a latent state ("vowels, One day I will tell your latent birth"‡).

---

*"*A,* black hairy corset of shiny flies." [Wherever C. L.-S. places emphasis on the poem's phonic values, I will leave the original French in the body of the text and place Fowlie's translation of Rimbaud in the footnotes. But where the emphasis is on the semantic content, the procedure will be reversed. Translator.]

†"Scarlet and black wounds break out on the proud flesh."

‡*Voyelles . . . je dirai quelque jour vos naissances latentes."*

What is more, Rimbaud explicitly points to the blackness of red in the lines from *Illuminations* cited and in other poems: "the black blood of belladonnas," "black purple color," "*ors vermeils*" rhyming with "*noirs sommeils*," "Black ugly one/Red-headed ugly one," "the red wash of the storm," "Reddened and their faces towards the black skies," and so on.*

Rimbaud was reading Baudelaire, for whom red, "such a dark, thick color," was similarly coupled with black: "ideal red . . . large night," "black night, red dawn," "the vast, black nothingness . . . the sun drowned in its blood."† Without having to invoke Stendhal, other examples could probably be found among the romantics and their successors; we may well be dealing with a cliché, whose bourgeois variant is perhaps the furniture of black wood covered in red velvet, so typical of the salons of the Second Empire and beyond.

That the phonetic symbolism of red shows through beneath the black, in the sonnet *Voyelles,* should be a stimulus to further analysis.

Phonologists have identified some sixteen to eighteen vowels in the French language, but Rimbaud was only aware of the five found in alphabet primers. The latter were recited and sung by schoolchildren with the soft pronunciation of the *e,* which Rimbaud saw as white ("the letter *e,* when non-accented, serves principally to write the vowel /ə/ termed the 'mute *e,*'" as Larousse's

---

*"*le sang noir des belladones,*" "*noirceurs purpurines,*" "red gold" and "black sleep," "*Noir Laideron/Roux Laideron,*" "*la toilette rouge de l'orage,*" "*Rougis et leurs fronts aux cieux noirs.*"

†"*cette couleur si obscure, si épaisse,*" "*rouge idéal . . . grande nuit,*" "*nuit noire, rouge aurore,*" "*néant vaste et noir . . . soleil noyé dans son sang.*"

Grand Dictionnaire des lettres notes). Now the mute *e* has been singled out by phonologists; for some of them, it is not a phoneme. In Jakobson's more penetrating analysis the mute *e* is the "zero-phoneme," and it is to be opposed, on the one hand, to all the other French phonemes (it has neither distinctive features nor constant sound characteristics), and on the other, to the absence of any phoneme.

The sonnet, then, implicitly recognizes the opposition, unique to the French language, between the /a/—the most chromatic and saturated of all phonemes—and the /ə/, the zero-phoneme. And this maximal phonological opposition is coupled with the opposition, also maximal but in panchromatic terms, between black and white. This latter opposition appears to predominate in Rimbaud, who under the influence of hashish speaks of "black moons, white moons"* (unlike the colored hallucinations of Théophile Gautier: "I heard the noises made by the colors. Green sounds, red, blue and yellow sounds came to me in perfectly distinct waves"†).

It would thus seem that Rimbaud's visual sensibility gave the advantage to luminance over chromatism, or, more precisely, that it placed the opposition of light and dark (generally considered the more archaic) before that of brightness and tonality—as seems to be the case in various exotic languages or cultures, notably in New Guinea, but also perhaps in Sanskrit, ancient Greek, and Old English.

The sonnet's third vowel is *i*, pictured as red. It is worth noting

---

*"*des lunes noires, des lunes blanches.*"

†"*J'entendais le bruit des couleurs. Des sons verts, rouges, bleus, jaunes m'arrivaient par ondes parfaitement distinctes.*" [My translation.]

that the first three vowels form the basic triangle of red, white, and black, which illustrates the double opposition between the presence or absence of brightness (black/white) and the presence or absence of tonality (red / black+white), with red, the color par excellence, occupying the apex.

After *i* or red comes *u,* which is green. Like the achromatic opposition black/white, the chromatic opposition red/green that follows is maximal. But this is not true in phonetics for the opposition between *i* and *u.* Here the maximal opposition, based on the axis of front and back vowels, would be that between *i* and the phoneme that in French is written as *ou*—but this latter vowel does not exist in the alphabet primers. As such, the most marked opposition Rimbaud had at his disposal was that between *i* and *u*—the latter being a rounded, palatal, front vowel, transcribed as /y/ by phoneticists, which occupies an intermediary position between the other two in the vocalic triangle.

Note that for Rimbaud the four colors considered so far form a system, which reappears in the sonnet to describe the first four vowels:

> "From your *black* Poems—Juggler!
> *White, green* and *red* dioptrics"*

Or again, from another poem:

> children reading in the flowering grass [*verdure*]
> their book of *red* morocco. Alas, he, like

De tes noirs Poèmes—Jongleur!
Blancs, verts, et rouges dioptriques

a thousand *white* angels separating on the road,
goes off beyond the mountain! She, all
cold and dark [*noire*], runs! after the departing man!*

(In the two quotes, I have emphasized the colors with italics.)

Last is *o* blue. In Rimbaud blue is not part of the four-term system, but it belongs to a two-term system that relates and opposes it to yellow: "blue and yellow Apotheosis," "Blue ugly one/Blond ugly one," "gold astral tears fell from blue heights," "Of blue Lotuses or Sunflowers," "The gold of Rios to the blue of the Rhine," "And the yellow and blue awakening of singing phosphorus," and "Lichens of sunlight and mucus of azure."[†]

As previously noted, neurologists have demonstrated that the oppositions red/green and blue/yellow belong to distinct neural channels, with the different ganglionic cells reacting to either one or the other. Now in the sonnet, yellow is missing: as only five vowels are considered, there is no room for a sixth color. Why Rimbaud chose blue over yellow is perhaps explained by the fact that blue is, after red, the most saturated color and would thus push yellow to the background. Castel already knew this and opposed the "insipidness" of yellow to "blue . . . of all the colors, the one

---

"des enfants lisant dans la verdure fleurie
leur livre de maroquin rouge! Hélas, Lui, comme
milles anges blancs qui se séparent sur la route,
s'éloigne par-delà la montagne! Elle, toute
froide et noire, court! après le départ de l'homme!"

[†]"*apothéose bleue et jaune,*" "*Bleu Laideron/Blond Laideron,*" "*des pleurs d'or astral tombaient des bleus degrés,*" "*De Lotos bleus ou d'Helianthes,*" "*L'or des Rios au bleu des Rhins,*" "*L'éveil jaune et bleu des phosphores chanteurs,*" "*Des lichens de soleil et des morves d'azur.*"

137

that rises highest, pure white being, it seems to me, simply a shade of blue." It is also possible that yellow's presence is latent, revealed only after blue (as red is present only beneath black in the poem's first verse). I am referring here to the "Clarion" [*Clairon*], and to the obvious etymology of the word ("yellow is clear [*clair*] by its nature," Castel said) and to this brass instrument's color (in French it is often called *cuivre jaune,* that is, literally, "yellow copper").

Rimbaud's mind probably offers fertile ground for the study of synesthesia. But when analyzing the poem, it would be wrong to consider each vowel separately relative to its corresponding color. *Voyelles* is not primarily an illustration of "colored hearing." As Castel would have understood, the sonnet is based on the homologies perceived between the differences. Even if one admits that Rimbaud's and Castel's sensitivity to black were similar, his verses do not claim that *a* is like black (as we saw, the perception of red is latent), or that *e* is like white, but—and this is something entirely different—that *a* as the fullest phoneme and *e* as the emptiest phoneme in the French language are as radically opposed to each other as the colors white and black. And if Rimbaud saw *i* as red and *u* as green, it was because, within the limits of his restricted vocalic repertoire, *i* is opposed to *u*, as a primary color to its complementary. It is not the immediately perceived sensory correspondences that reveal the sonnet's architecture, but the relations between these correspondences as established unconsciously by the understanding.

There can be no doubt that Rimbaud's poetry employs a very large number of color words, and it is difficult to avoid the impression that he often used them as padding. Still, it is not without consequence that these words were the preferred reservoir from which he drew to complete his verses. And he did not choose just any colors (except perhaps for *"vert-chou,"* which is not easily explained, except as a rhyme for *"caoutchouc"* and *"acajou"*—though one might note that, according to neurologists, the yellow and blue poles lean toward chartreuse and violet). Rimbaud possessed a cerebral color map that was particularly fertile and highly practicable.

Let us not neglect the abundance of nasal consonants. Chabanon, it would appear, described the sonnet's phonetic structure a century in advance, when speaking of nasal syllables: "These ungrateful sounds, cleverly slipped in among more vivid sounds [the vowels!] forming, as with shadows and masses, the chiaroscuro of language." One is reminded of *Une saison en enfer* ("I invented the color of the vowels! . . . I regulated the form and movement of each consonant"*) and feels obliged to inquire into the sonnet's consonantism, which is so rich in diffuse consonants, as accented by the use of alliteration and paronymy: *bombinent, puanteurs; ombre; candeur des vapeurs; fiers, blancs, ombelles; pourpres, lèvres belles; ivresses pénitentes; vibrements divins, mers virides, paix de pâtis, paix des rides. . .* Jakobson noted somewhere that nasality is "most compatible with the unmarked members of the compact/diffuse opposition, that is, with diffuseness in consonants, and with compactness in vowels." I do not have the necessary competence to push the linguistic analysis any further.

Finally, one should note that the vowels suggest sounds, whether directly or indirectly, as well as colors. The flies of *a* buzz, *e* evokes quivering, *i* laughter, *u* vibrations, and *o* both harsh, high-pitched sounds and silence. Thus one moves from continuous noise (buzzing) to discontinuous tremulousness (quivering), followed by periodic agitation (cycles, vibrations), finally arriving at an alternance of violent noises (stridors) and silence. The latter, at the poem's end, corresponds, in the acoustic register,

---

*"A Season in Hell": "*J'inventai la couleur des voyelles! . . . Je réglai la forme et le mouvement de chaque consonne.*"

to the joint presence at the beginning of black and red (the latter in a state of latency) in the visual register. Similarly, in the last line,

—O the Omega, violet beam from His Eyes!*

the blue dissolves by blending with red ("violet is a somber color," Castel wrote) as if to draw to a close the series that began with black. Or again, it is as if *o*'s acoustic ambiguity, along with its visual lean toward violet, reproduces in the form of a chiasmus the visual ambiguity of *a*, together with the absence of acoustic ambiguity denoted by the continuous buzzing.

Voyelles

A noir, E blanc, I rouge, U vert, O bleu: voyelles
Je dirai quelque jour vos naissances latentes:
A, noir corset velu des mouches éclatantes
Qui bombinent autour des puanteurs cruelles,

Golfes d'ombre; E, candeurs des vapeurs et des tentes
Lances des glaciers fiers, rois blancs, frissons d'ombelles;
I, pourpres, sang craché, rire des lèvres belles
Dans la colère ou les ivresses pénitentes;

U, cycles, vibrements divins des mers virides,
Paix des pâtis semés d'animaux, paix des rides
Que l'alchimie imprime aux grands fronts studieux;

----

*—O l'Oméga, rayon violet de Ses Yeux!

O, suprême Clairon plein des strideurs étranges,
Silences traversés des Mondes et des Anges:
—O l'Oméga, rayon violet de Ses Yeux!*

---

*Vowels
A black, E white, I red, U green, O blue: vowels,
One day I will tell your latent birth:
A, Black hairy corset of shining flies
Which buzz around cruel stench,

Gulfs of darkness; E, whiteness of vapors and tents,
Lances of proud glaciers, white kings, quivering of flowers;
I, purples, spit blood, laughter of beautiful lips
In anger or penitent drunkenness;

U, cycles, divine vibrations of grean seas,
Peace of pastures scattered with animals, peace of the wrinkles
Which alchemy prints on heavy studious brows;

O, supreme Clarion full of strange stridor,
Silences crossed by worlds and angels:
—O the Omega, violet beam from His Eyes!

20

I have spoken elsewhere of how I first came to know André Breton. It was on a long boat ride to Martinique, during which, in order to relieve our boredom and discomfort, we discussed the nature of the work of art, first in writing, then in conversation.

I began by submitting a long note to André Breton. He responded, and I have treasured his letter ever since. Chance had it that, much later, I found my own note while classifying old papers. Breton had probably returned it to me.

Here it is, followed by André Breton's unpublished text (which I wish to thank Madame Elisa Breton and Madame Aube Elléouët for giving me permission to publish).

A commentary on the relation between works of art and documents, written and delivered to André Breton on board the Capitaine Paul-Lemerle *in March 1941*

Claude Lévi-Strauss

In the *Manifeste du surréalisme,** A.B. defined artistic creation in terms of the absolutely spontaneous activity of the mind; such activity may well result from systematic training and the methodical application of a certain number of prescripts; nevertheless the work of art is defined—and defined exclusively—by its total liberty. It seems that on this point, A.B. has modified his position appreciably (in *La Situation surréaliste de l'objet*†). However, the relation that, according to him, exists between the work of art and the document is not perfectly clear. If it is obvious that every work of art is a document, does this imply, as suggested by a radical interpretation of his thesis, that every document is therefore a work of art? Starting from the position of the *Manifesto,* three interpretations are, in truth, possible:

- The artwork's aesthetic value depends exclusively on the degree of its spontaneity: the most valuable work (as a work of art) is defined by the absolute liberty of its production. As everyone, once suitably trained, is capable of attaining this complete liberty of expression, poetic production is open to all. The work's documentary value merges with its aesthetic value; the best document (as judged by its degree of creative spontaneity) is also the best poem. In principle, if not in fact, the best poem can not only be understood, but produced by anybody. One could then conceive of a humanity in which everyone, being trained in a sort of cathartic method, would be a poet.

  Such an interpretation would abolish all the ascriptive

* *Manifesto of Surrealism.*

† *Surrealist Situation of the Object.*

privileges implied until now by the term *talent*. And if this interpretation does not deny the role of work and effort in artistic creation, it relegates them, at the very least, to the stage prior to creation proper—that of the difficult search for and application of the methods required to sustain free thought.

- One can maintain the preceding interpretation but nevertheless note, a posteriori, that if all the works obtained from a large number of individuals are equivalent from a documentary point of view (that is, they all result from equally authentic and spontaneous mental activity), they are not at all equivalent from an artistic point of view, as some of them give pleasure, whereas others do not. As long as the work of art is defined as a document (that is, as any product of the mind's activity), one can admit the distinction without attempting to explain it (and without having the dialectics to do so). One will simply note that some individuals are poets and others are not, despite the fact that the conditions underlying their productions are exactly the same. Every work of art will still be a document, but there is room to distinguish between those that are also works of art and those that are just documents. As both are still defined as products of the mind, the distinction, being established only a posteriori, will have to be considered a primitive given, which, by definition, escapes all interpretation. The specificity of the work of art will be recognized without being able to be explained. It will become a "mystery."

- Finally, the third interpretation, while still maintaining the fundamental principle of the irreducibly irrational and spontaneous character of artistic creation, distinguishes between the document, the raw product of mental activity, and the work of art, which always involves an element of secondary elaboration. It is obvious, however, that such elaboration cannot be the work of rational and critical thought; the very possibility must be radically excluded. But it can be supposed that, under certain conditions and among certain people, spontaneous irrational thought may well become conscious of itself and become truly reflective —its being understood that such reflection is carried out in accordance with its own norms, and that these norms are as impermeable to rational analysis as the matter to which they are applied. This "irrational intellection" leads to a certain elaboration of the raw material as expressed in the choices, omissions, and arrangement, themselves a function of mandatory structures. If every work of art remains a document, as a work of art it transcends the documentary level, not just in terms of the quality of its raw expressiveness, but in terms of the value of its secondary elaboration. The latter, moreover, is "secondary" only in relation to the mind's basic automatic functioning; relative to rational, critical thought, it presents the same irreducible, primitive character as the automatisms themselves.

The first interpretation does not accord with the facts; the second removes the problem of artistic creation from theoretical analysis. The third alone seems capable of avoiding a certain confusion (from which surrealism does not always appear to have escaped) between what is or is not, or is more or less, aesthetically valuable. All documents are not necessarily works of art, and all that constitutes a break may be equally valuable to the psychologist or militant, but not to the poet, even if the poet is also a militant. The work of someone mentally deficient has a documentary interest equal to the work of Lautréamont; it may even have greater polemical value. But the one is a work of art and the other is not, and there must be the dialectical means to account for their difference, just as one must also be able to account for the possibility that Picasso is a greater painter than Braque, that Apollinaire is a great poet and Roussel is not, or that Salvador Dali is a great painter but an appalling writer. Judgments of this type, though they may differ from or be contrary to my own—and the judgments given here are only examples*—constitute the absolutely necessary conclusion to the dialectic between the poet and the theorist.

Since we have recognized that the fundamental conditions of the production of the document and the work of art are identical, these essential distinctions can only be acquired by displacing the analysis from the production to the product, and from the artist to his or her work.

On rereading this handwritten commentary today, I am troubled by the awkwardness of its thought, as well as the heavy-handedness of its expression. It is a weak excuse, but clearly it was written in a single sitting (there are only two words crossed out). I would have preferred had it been forgotten. But that would do an injustice to the important text that Breton wrote in response. Without my piece, one would not understand what his was about.

---

*Even formulated in hypothetical terms, these judgments strike me today as quite naive. Luckily, my horizons of 1941 would be expanded by contact with the surrealists.

In Breton's manuscript, there are around ten words or phrases that, having been carefully crossed out, cannot be deciphered; they have been replaced by new wording in the space between the lines, which also contains several additions. The large number of corrections made to the last lines does not permit one to judge whether Breton, if less pressed for time, would have opted for a more grammatically correct construction, or whether he rejected the latter deliberately.

The response of André Breton

The fundamental contradiction that you are pointing to has not escaped my attention: it remains despite my efforts, and those of several others, to reduce it (but this doesn't really worry me because I realize that it contains the secret to that forward movement on which surrealism's survival depends). Yes, naturally, my positions have varied considerably since the first manifesto. One should understand that in such programmatic texts, which do not tolerate the expression of any doubt or reservation, and whose essentially aggressive character excludes all nuance, my thought tends to take on an extremely brutal, that is, simplistic character foreign to its real nature.

The contradiction that you find so striking is the same one, I believe, that Caillois reacted so strongly to (I told you about this). I have tried to respond in a text entitled "*La Beauté sera convulsive*" (*Minotaure*, no. 5) and reprinted at the beginning of *L'Amour fou*. Indeed, I find myself pulled in two very different directions—and after all, why not? for I am not alone in this respect. The first leads me to search for the pleasure the work of art gives (the word "pleasure,"* which you used, is the only really appropriate word, for when I consider my own reactions, they appear to me as para-erotic). The second, which may or may not manifest itself independently of the first, leads me to interpret the work of art as a function of the general need for knowledge. These two impulses, which I am distinguishing on paper, cannot always be easily separated (they tend, for example, to merge in many a passage of *Une Saison en enfer*).

It goes without saying that, if every work of art can be considered from a documentary perspective, the converse is by no means true.

On examining your three interpretations one after the other, I have no difficulty in telling you that I feel close only to the last one. A few words, however, regarding the first two:

• I am not certain that a work's *aesthetic* value depends on its degree of spontaneity. I was much more concerned with its authenticity than its beauty and the definition of 1924 testifies to this: "A dictate of thought . . . beyond any *aesthetic* or moral preoccupation." It cannot have escaped your notice that, had I omitted this last part of the sentence, I would have deprived the authors of automatic texts of a part of their liberty. It was imperative that, from the beginning, they be sheltered from all such judgments, if one hoped to prevent them from being subjected to any a priori constraint, and acting accordingly. This, unfortunately, has not always been the case (in my letter to Rolland de Reneville, published in *Point du jour,* I deplored the minimal alterations required to turn an automatic text into a

---

*The word is *la jouissance* in the original. [Translator's note.]

poem—but it is easy to proclaim one's concerns while abstracting them from the work under consideration).

• I am not so sure as you that large qualitative differences exist between the various texts obtained by entirely spontaneous means. It has always appeared to me that the *main* reason why so many of these texts are so mediocre is that many people find it impossible to place themselves in the conditions necessary for the experience. They are satisfied with a rambling, disconnected discourse which, with its absurdities and sudden shifts in subject-matter, gives them the illusion of success; but the signs are easily detected which suggest that they haven't really "gotten their feet wet," and that their supposed authenticity is a bit of a sham. If I say that I am not so sure as you, it is largely because I do not understand how the *self* (which is common to all) is distributed among different individuals (whether equally or, if unequally, to what degree?). Only a systematic investigation, and one that provisionally leaves artists aside, can teach us anything about this matter. But I am hardly interested in establishing a hierarchy of surrealist works (contrary to Aragon who once said: "If you write dreadful rubbish in an authentically surrealistic manner, it is still rubbish")—nor, as I have made clear, a hierarchy of romantic or symbolist works. It is not just that my classification of the latter would be fundamentally different from those now current; my major reason for objecting to these classifications is that they cause us to lose sight of these movements' profound, historical significance.

• Does the work of art *always* require secondary elaboration? Yes, undoubtedly, but only in the very broad sense you give it when speaking of "irrational intellection"—though one wonders at what level of consciousness this elaboration occurs? We, at any rate, would still be in the pre-conscious. Shouldn't the productions of Hélène Smith, when in a trance state, be considered works of art? And if someone demonstrated that certain of Rimbaud's poems were simply day dreams, would you enjoy them less? Or would you relegate them to the drawer labeled "documents"? I still find the distinction arbitrary. And it becomes positively specious in my eyes when you oppose the poet Apollinaire to the "non-poet" Roussel, or the painter Dali to the writer Dali. Are you sure that the first of these judgments is not too traditional, that it is not indebted to an antiquated conception of poetry? I do not consider Dali a great "painter," for the excellent reason that his technique is manifestly regressive. With Dali, it is truly the man that interests me, and his poetic interpretation of the world. Again, I cannot associate myself with your conclusion (but you already knew this). I have other, more pressing reasons for not accepting it. These reasons, I insist, are of a *practical nature* (adhesion to the mater. histor.). If a loosening of psychological responsibility is necessary to obtain the initial state on which everything depends, so be it, but afterwards, responsibility, both psychological and moral. The progressive identification of the conscious "me" with the totality of its concretions (this is badly put), understood as the theater within which the self is called on to produce and reproduce itself. A tendency to synthesize the pleasure principle with the reality principle (I must be excused for still remaining at the limits of my thinking on this matter); the agreement at any price between the art work and the extra-artistic behavior. Anti-valéryism.

2 1

When writing the end of *The Naked Man,* I was thinking of the final grandiose page of the *Essay on the Inequality of the Human Races.* In it Gobineau evoked the inevitable disappearance of our species, an outcome about which there can be no doubt since "Science, . . . while revealing our beginnings, has seemed to assure us that we must also reach an end." There will come, he continued, "an age of death when the earth, silent and without us, will continue to describe its impassive orbits in space."

The tone of the piece and the epithet *impassive* had remained engraved in my memory. It inspired me. But at the same time, another adjective, but not drawn from Gobineau, came to me with singular force—*abrogated,* used to qualify *evidence.**

---

*The word *cancelled* has been substituted for *abrogated* in the English translation of *The Naked Man.* The passage reads: "Although he can never at any moment lose sight of the opposite certainty that he was not present on earth in former times, that he will

I was well aware that the word was inappropriate. Abrogation is an act of a public power. One abrogates a law or ruling; one does not abrogate evidence: the latter is discussed, disputed, invalidated. . . And yet I was irresistibly compelled to write *abrogated.*

The reason for this incongruity only appeared to me several years later, when I was led (I no longer remember the exact circumstances) to reread this page of Gobineau. In imitating it—from a distance, it is true, so that the resemblance could easily pass unnoticed—I retained the word *impassive,* which qualified *orb* in Gobineau,* but I balked at using this last word, for fear of introducing a precious and rather anachronistic note into my text.

But the word *orb,* though repressed, did not entirely disappear. Having undergone a transformation similar, if on a much smaller scale, to those one observes in myths, its phonic characteristics reemerged from under my pen, but in inverted form: *abrogated* contains *b, r, o,* instead of *o, r, b.* As soon as I perceived this, it became obvious why I had, seemingly, been compelled to choose an incongruous word; for this choice exemplifies one of the mechanisms of literary creation. An impropriety is no longer improper when it possesses its own logic—a logic that differs from that of the discourse in which it is first introduced. It is perceived, instead, as an original use of language that gives the expression a cer-

---

not always be here in the future and that, with his inevitable disappearance from the surface of a planet which is itself doomed to die, his labours, his joys, his hopes and his works will be as if they had never existed, since no consciousness will survive to preserve even the memory of these ephemeral phenomena, only a few features of which, soon to be erased from the impassive face of the earth, will remain as already *cancelled evidence* that they once were, and were as nothing." [Translator's note and emphasis.]

*The word in the original French is *orbe* and not *orbite,* as the English translation suggests. [Translator's note.]

tain bite. Having been deflected from its proper meaning, the word acquires an unfamiliar signification, which the author had not intended. He or she may notice it, but without realizing that this semantic innovation was due to causes that have nothing to do with conscious thought.

Regarding Objects

22

In the history of the plastic arts, did realism come before convention or was it the reverse? The subject was fashionable at the turn of the century, but according to Boas it is a false problem.

> Since both of these tendencies are active in the human mind at the present time, it seems much more likely that both processes have been at work constantly, and that neither the one nor the other theory really represents the historical development of decorative design.

To be sure. Nonetheless, it is rather perplexing to see Boas, in his famous study of the needle cases of the Alaskan Inuit, show how, in page after page, recent sculptors have delighted in giving a realist turn to conventional forms that had existed, the evidence suggests, since prehistoric times from the Bering Strait all the way to Greenland. At the same time, Boas avoids the "entirely obscure" problem of the origin of these conventional forms, which cannot be explained in technical or utilitarian terms. Like much of the art of the American Northwest, these forms evoke animal figures, but often they are so highly stylized as to be unrecognizable.

Behind the false problem denounced by Boas, a different problem lies hidden. The art of preliterate peoples does not just refer to nature or convention, or even to both together; it also refers to the supernatural. We have replaced the supernatural, which we no longer see directly, with conventional symbols or ennobled human figures. Elsewhere, in Melanesia or, for example, the American Northwest coast, conventional representations play a role, but they do not take the place of experience. They provide a sort of grammar, whose rules, when applied (whether consciously or unconsciously), express a lived reality.

The language of California's Wintu Indians distinguished between beliefs and experiential truths. When speaking of the supernatural, they always used the grammatical forms relating to experience, whereas those events or phenomena that have a natural causality were placed among the things that are known only indirectly and impersonally.

One of the myths of the Oglala Sioux, from the American Plains, has as its heroine a young woman who is all the more perfect for having come from the beyond.

> She could dress skins so that they were white and soft, and from them make good clothing, upon which she put beautiful ornaments and each ornament meant something.
>
> On the sides of [her son's] moccasins [young women commanded by her] put mountains so that he could step from hill to hill without touching the valleys; on the tops they put dragon flies so that he could escape all danger; on his leggings they put wolf tracks so that he would never grow weary; on his shirt they put the tipi circle so that he would find shelter everywhere.

Anyone familiar with the art of the Sioux knows that their motifs, generally geometrical designs, are quite remote from nature (to the point where the informants tended to interpret them each in his or her own way). They were, however, supposed to represent realities beyond ordinary experience.

One can also, in a sense, apply the problem discussed by Boas to music, in which case popular music would be to highbrow music as decorative art is to representative art. In both cases, the first term on either side of the equation is closely associated with a supporting role, that is to say, an object's decoration is like a dance's musical accompaniment. Both, moreover, proceed by the composition and repetition of simple elements—verses and refrains on the one hand, recurrent patterns on the other. And the content of both is impoverished, with the same prevalence of empty stylistic forms, the same gratuitous character.

Popular music antedates highbrow music. One is thus tempted, on the basis of this analogy, to think that decorative art also appeared first. The parallelism, however, does not hold true: the problem is that, in order to develop, music, unlike the plastic arts, had to establish a system of notation or writing, with which to mediate between conception and execution. In its break with oral tradition, it was imperative that music could be written down so that it could become representative—representative, that is, of itself, and not of something else. (Kant did not like music: he considered it the least of the fine arts and faulted it with, among other things, disturbing the neighbors. Yet music too fits his definition of art as purposiveness without purpose.)

Oral expression has produced great works without writing: one thinks of myths, Homeric poems, and medieval epics, all of which were first confided to memory alone. Why does music need writing, let alone its own form of writing? No doubt because, whereas oral literature can employ language, considered as an instrument of general usage, music requires a language appropriate to it—though the latter can never be entirely appropriate, given the opposition between the continuity of musical discourse and the discontinuity that inheres in every system of notation.

Art can be considered as "primitive" in one of two senses. First, in the sense that the artist does not have sufficient grasp of the technical means or know-how necessary to realize his or her objective (that is, the imitation of a model), and as such can only signify it; an example would be what we call "naive" art. In the second sense, the model the artist would depict, being supernatural, necessarily escapes any naturalistic means of representation: again the artist can only signify, but as a result of the object's excess, and not the subject's shortcomings. The art of preliterate peoples, in all its different forms, illustrates the latter case.

Now, so-called high-brow music possesses both elements concurrently. During modern times in the West, and at various times in other literate cultures, such music emancipated itself from popular music (which, as it remains tied to other activities, contributes to structure without constituting it). However, even as high-brow music attained a certain autonomy, its subjection to the sort of constraints associated with both "primitive" art and the art of "primitives" was to become all the more manifest. There is the same inadequacy of the means relative to the end, due, on the one hand, to the system of writing inherited from the past, which, with its discontinuous signs, has resisted all the attempts at reform proposed during the last few centuries (the score does not represent the music, but only signifies it), and, on the other hand, to the musical instruments required to carry out the composer's intentions: these instruments (and ultimately, they are just machines), though also inherited from the past, have throughout the course of the centuries become increasingly complex without, however, having been able to overcome fully all the concrete problems associated with the resistance of their materials, their construction, acoustics, temperature, and humidity with which the musician, however skillful, will have to come to terms.*

All this concerns only the first element. The second applies not just to a particular historical state of music, but to the art of music in general. Unlike articulate speech, music lacks a vocabulary connoting the givens of sense experience. Consequently, the universe to which it refers cannot be represented, and for this reason music has—but here in a literal sense—a supernatural reality. As music is composed of sounds and chords that do not exist in nature, the ancients placed it in close proximity to the gods.

Given these characteristics, and given the slowness, relative to the other arts, with which music conquered its autonomy, it remains for us—however paradoxical this may sound—a "primitive" art. The surrealists were almost all deaf to music. Could the reason for this lie not so much with this art (which, like the other arts they admired, is primitive), as with the fact that, in music, they did not find anything to oppose, in contrast to painting and poetry, many of whose productions they despised? The absence of an adversary rendered them helpless.

It has often been the case in the history of art that, as the technical knowledge and skill increase, the aesthetic quality declines. Many examples could be provided, from ancient Egypt down to the present. Nonetheless, art and impeccable craftsmanship sometimes appear together, as with Ingres. But then Ingres (an exemplary case, to which I continually return) consciously renounced

---

*The original uses the verb *composer* [*avec*], which I have translated as "to come to terms with." In French *composer* means both "to write," "to draw up," and to "compromise" or "come to terms with." C. L.-S. explicitly draws attention to the "revealing ambiguity of the term," an ambiguity that, alas, proves untranslatable in English. [Translator's note.]

(with what Delacroix criticized as a lack of naïveté) what was at the time considered to be technical progress: chiaroscuro and relief (or else returning to the procedure, then described as "gothic," of modeling with light). He took pride in using "the schools of the fourteenth and fifteenth centuries . . . with greater effect than they [his detractors] could ever imagine." Hence he was reproached, like Poussin, with archaism.

Consider the following as an example of the kind of problem that preoccupied Boas in his pioneering reflections on the art of preliterate peoples: a pair of leggings of the Thompson Indians of British Columbia have leather fringes; some of these are left plain, others decorated with strings of beads made of either glass or bone; and they are arranged such that bone fringes alternate with glass fringes, and beaded fringes with nonbeaded ones. Now Boas notes that when the leggings are worn, the fringes become entangled, even when the person wearing them is not moving. The woman who made them could not have been all that concerned with how they would look. Her calculations, and the care she took to ensure that they were respected, must have had as their sole source the pleasure she derived from their execution. The decorative rhythm at the source of the costume's beauty, says Boas, is similar in nature to dance steps, or the repetitive motions demanded by many technical activities, or, more generally, the regular rhythms of certain motor habits (such as swaying the arms while walking).

For Boas (as already for Diderot) regularity, symmetry, and rhythm are at the basis of all aesthetic activity. However, his formalism prevents him from admitting that the (direct or indirect) imitation of physical or bodily compulsions has its source in the emotions or conveys a message. The emotive charge, when it exists, is a mere add-on. No doubt, Boas was right to proscribe the sentimental or philosophical verbiage that too often passes for art criticism. But it is ironic that his formalism should seek, in movements and gestures, a naturalist or empirical foundation for the arts. Between the two extremes, one could, as was once said of the melody and the bass in Grétry's harmony, drive a carriage.

One has only to consider Boas's detailed analysis of the arrangement of patterns and colors in Peruvian textiles (and in clothing or finery made of other materials) for the real nature of decorative rhythms to become evident. The latter always implies a *combinatoire,* with which is associated a certain intellectual satisfaction.

Benveniste has demonstrated that in Greek the original meaning of *rhuthmos* was "the characteristic arrangements of the parts in a whole." With Plato the word's spatial connotation became temporal and was extended to the bodily movements of gymnastics and dancing. Boas, like his contemporaries, reversed the proper etymological order by deriving rhythm, understood in a spatial sense, from essentially temporal physiological motor phenomena. The pre-Socratics were right to believe that in decorative rhythm the idea of the "whole" prevails, for recurrence is only perceptible if the rhythmic cell contains a limited number of elements. How is an order established among a finite set of elements obtained at random, or among the disparate objects the *bricoleur* finds in his treasure trove? The idea of rhythm encompasses the series of permutations required to turn a collection into a system. This holds true for the materials and forms, the colors and durations, for the accents or timbres, as well as for orientations in both time and space.

Periodicity, whether temporal or spatial, has a role to play, for repetition is essential to symbolic expression. The symbol coincides intuitively with its object without ever becoming identical to it. Relative to the thing symbolized, the symbol forms a whole whose elements are different from those present in the thing, but

Claude Lévi-Strauss

between the elements of the two sets there exist the same relations. Accordingly, in order for the symbol to be durably confirmed as such, it has to acquire a physical connection with the thing: thus whenever the circumstances are the same, the symbol must be regularly repeated.

Wagner permuted the five different durations assigned to five successive notes, thus creating the leitmotives for Brünhilde's Sleep, the Bird, and the Daughters of the Rhine. Other variations were possible; perhaps someday someone will identify them. But whether this happens or not, one would still like to understand why in the mind of the composer certain permutations formed a system, and others did not. The same applies to the distribution of beads on a necklace or fringe, or the designs and colors of a fabric. Any number of arrangements could have satisfied the need for regularity, symmetry, and rhythm. The problem, then, is not whether regularity, symmetry, and rhythm exist, but why the artist chose this rhythm or that pattern, rather than some other. One must seek elsewhere for the solution to the problem posed by the presence of decorative rhythms.

Even among the so-called primitive arts, some of them go further than others in the search for structure. African art generally limits itself to stylizing. There is certainly structural transposition, but it tends to be at a plastic level. Its structure is, one might say, the one immediately subjacent to reality, or the one closest to the empirical object. Thus it is not surprising that black African art was the first to be discovered by Western art in its search for renewal, but it is also the most limited.

In this search some theories of art also go further than others. When a theory consciously inspires an art or artwork the results tend to be even more tiresome. If a durable style is to appear, it is imperative that the artist not, in his zeal for some intellectual schema, try to step over the distance between the world and the manner of its representation. Around 1920 it seems that Darius Milhaud deliberately composed fugues according to some natural law. And when Marcel Duchamp painted his *Nu descendant un escalier*,* he was referring consciously to the technique of chronophotography. Such works soon betray their lack of substance, for their significance proves to be exhausted by the very act of their expression.

On the other hand, when heraldic art first depicted crowns, no one would have realized that their forms replicated those of extremely fleeting states of matter. An earl's crown offers an exact image of the splash caused by a drop of milk as it lands in a glass of milk, but this could not be known until the invention of chronophotography. Similarly, those who conceived of what are called "close" royal or imperial crowns were not aware—and for good reason—that their prototype, which nature had long kept secret, is generated for a fraction of a second by the explosion of an atomic bomb.

Though the original artists could not have realized it, the crowns result from an intuitive apperception (which for all the world resembles divination) of matter's unstable states. What is all the more remarkable is that the ranking of crowns reproduces what, according to modern physics, are the degrees of matter's instability in the transition from liquid to gas. The human mind was capable of conceiving these forms and their relations long before their real existence had been revealed.

Nude Descending a Staircase.

23

We do not hold basket making in very high regard. It does not have a place of honor in our museums alongside painting and sculpture, or even furniture or the applied arts. Already by the eighteenth century, basketry appeared destined for oblivion, as the following prescient judgment from the *Encyclopédie* attests:

> This is quite an ancient and useful art; the desert fathers and pious hermits practiced it in their refuges, and derived from it much of their subsistence. Formerly it provided fine pieces to serve at the tables of magnates, but one scarcely sees them anymore, for they have been replaced by crystal.

Who today among French speakers would still recognize the words *mandrerie, closerie, faisserie,* and *lasserie,* which designated the four principal techniques of the art of basket making?

Basketry, another encyclopedia will note a century later, "employs primary materials that are amply provided by nature and require minimal preparation; and the fashioning of these materials demands only a certain manual dexterity, and little or no tools." Moreover, the products of this art are perishable. All this helps explain why it has fallen into disfavor.

Among preliterate peoples, by contrast, this art occupies a place of the utmost importance; it lent itself to innumerable uses and attained a perfection that we can no longer equal. In the hands of specialists, basketry constituted a noble art that among the Plains Indians, for example, was the privilege of a circle of initiates.

Yet the beliefs and rites of these peoples reveal a certain ambivalence to basket making. In North America the most wonderful basket makers lived west of the Rockies, in California, Oregon, British Columbia, and Alaska. According to one of their myths a successful basket had to satisfy two requirements: it had to be perfectly watertight (in this region where there was little or no pottery, coiled baskets, stitched together extremely tightly, served as recipients for water and other liquids; stones heated on the fire were plunged into them to cook food); and it had to bear in its coils a decorative pattern like the one revealed to the first basket maker when she saw the play of the sun's rays on the brook.

Thus the myth places the functional and what we would call the decorative dimension on the same plane. But is the word *decorative* appropriate? The myths of California's Pomo Indians suggest otherwise.

The basket spirits, they claimed, live within the decorative coils; it is their village. And within the latter there must be a "door," that is, an intentionally created defect, that, often scarcely visible, breaks the continuity of the design and allows the basket spirits, when they die, to escape and ascend to their sky home. One woman who failed to make a "door" on her basket, was condemned to death by the imprisoned spirit. The World Maker, feeling sorry for her, consented that the basket maker and basket spirit could rise to the sky together.

It was not uncommon for manufactured objects to be inhabited by spirits. That special exits had to be prepared for them implies that they were particularly exposed. It could be said that baskets represent a particularly unstable state of equilibrium between nature and culture. They are close to nature in that nature provides ample materials requiring little or no preparation; their manufacture requires little work (I shall qualify this presently); and because their time of service is limited, they are fated to end up on the rubbish heap. On the other hand, baskets are temporarily integrated into culture by the fact of their manufacture and usage.

When in the bush or forest, I often saw an Indian, in order to carry wild plants or game, cut down a palm branch, smooth down its leaflets, and weave them right then and there. He had thereby made a basket, but one that would be discarded as soon as he returned to camp; there would be no further use for such improvised packaging. This, no doubt, is the extreme case, particularly when compared with the masterpieces of coiled basketry found in North America, which are stitched rather than woven, take an experienced worker several days to manufacture, and often last well beyond the generation that made them. But among these peoples, one also finds far less durable, flexible baskets employed to hold their domestic effects.

The numerous small populations established in the region did not all make the same kinds of baskets, and their use varied from one group to another. Yet despite this diversity, it seems that in the area stretching from Oregon to British Columbia, baskets were divided into two categories: hard and soft—an opposition that the Thompson language (of the Salish family) renders nicely by way of a phonetic contrast: *kwetskwetsä'ist* for hard, stiff basketry and *lepalepä'ist* for soft or flexible basketry.

Mythology also gives expression to this opposition. The Indians of the Sahaptian language speak of the Soft-Basket People, thieving ogresses and child eaters. Among the neighboring Chinook, an analogous figure exists in the person of the "Basket Ogress," who is designated by the same name in Upper Chinook as the Soft-Basket People in Sahaptian. The Salish of Puget Sound—who also speak of a dangerous basket people—refer to this same character as the Snail Woman because, after her death, her basket turns into the shell of a snail. To crush such a shell turns one into a cannibal. These Indians describe with considerable precision the construction of the ogress's basket, which is similar to those that they carry to dig for clams and has to be sufficiently strong to lend itself to such harsh work.

Myths relate how the World Maker, the Trickster, or else a cultural hero caused one of these ogresses to die in a fire or by some other means. Several other kinds of baskets are hostile, if to a lesser degree, and form the retinue of these cannibals. According to a Pomo myth (and the Pomo, it will be remembered, arranged a door in the decorative coils of the baskets for the departure of the basket spirits), the Trickster met with the Basket People ("all kinds of baskets, and they were human"). As they refused him any service and "would not remain where he placed them," the furious Trickster smashed them to pieces. The Chehalis, or coastal Salish, tell how in times past their cultural hero was upset with the basket men: the latter could walk, but on reaching the heights of the mountain they would let themselves fall all the way back to the river, where the dried fish with which they were filled would come back to life and swim away. The hero decreed that from then on baskets could no longer move by themselves, and that humans would have to take the trouble to carry them and their load.

Throughout the American Northwest, the motif of cannibal

baskets is closely associated with that of the ogress who is killed in the cause of her own beautification (the child she has captured persuades her to undergo a treatment that will make her as white, or as prettily striped, or as capable of making delightful sounds as her would-be victim, but this treatment, of course, proves fatal). This latter motif is common in the so-called low cultures of South America, notably that of the Gê, and leads one to wonder whether there are South American parallels to the basket myths.

In North America, among the Sahaptin, the Soft-Basket Lady is not only an ogress, she seduces men and cuts off their penises with her toothed vagina. In South America, the Guarani story of Genesis collected by Leon Cadogan relates, among other events, how the Demiurge turned a basket into a woman that he adopted as his daughter. He gave her in marriage to the ogre Charia, and the latter, on the way back to his village, decided to sleep with her, an act that left his penis in shreds. Charia beat the woman, and she immediately resumed the form of a basket. Though the text does not explicitly say so, one can assume that, like the North American Basket Lady, she had a toothed vagina. A Guayaki version of the Guarani Genesis (gathered by Pierre Clastres, but whose authenticity he considers questionable) tells of how the Sun was saved by an ogre from a trap in which it had been caught. The Sun then wove a basket and transformed it into a woman with whom he rewarded the ogre, but not without warning him not to take her too often to bathe. The ogre neglected the advice, and the woman disappeared in the water to reemerge some distance away as a basket.

From this story, Clastres infers that the Guayaki saw the basket as a metonym for woman. Such a conclusion is a little hasty, for in a myth of the Amazonian Tupi, close cousins to the Guarani, a basket is transformed into a jaguar (whose spotted coat recalls the basket's meshes, but this too does not provide a sufficient explanation)—and the jaguar is a homicidal animal, not unlike the woman with the toothed vagina.

The suspect Guayaki version may have, moreover, a more explicit counterpart among the Pomo of California, whom I have already mentioned on several occasions. In this myth the second, more finely decorated of two baskets was thrown into a lake by Frog and Coyote when it was only half-finished. The basket became a demon and caused any menstruating woman who saw it to fall sick. Thus, from one end of the New World to the other, one can detect several states of the same transformation. A Basket Lady who bloodies men's genitalia and thus makes them ill becomes a Basket Lord who causes women with already bloodied genitalia to become ill. And in both Paraguay and California, an incompletely metamorphosed basket (whether into a woman by a man, or into a finished product by a woman) must not be put into water—even though in California at least, one must be able to put water into a basket to prove the worth of its construction.

South American myths, like those of North America, are acquainted with malevolent basket peoples. In Bolivia the Tacana Indians relate how the baskets became upset at their inconsiderate treatment by humans, who, when they were no longer of any use, threw them to the animals, or even into the fire. The baskets decided to dump their loads and flee to the jungle. Humans no longer knew where to put their things, and their provisions lay scattered all over the ground. Eventually, the baskets were moved by this disorder and returned to the village.

Obviously these myths have a kinship with all those about objects that rise up against their masters; the latter are also told by the Tacana, but older versions are known to have existed in the Andes and among the Maya. However, the objects in revolt are generally rigid and hard. Pottery, millstones, mortars, and stone pestles (in other versions, dogs and other domesticated animals) reproach humans for their cruelty and form alliances to exterminate them. In *Popol Vuh,* the sacred book of the Maya, this is how the first creation ends, and a new humanity has to be created. The last cutters and polishers of stone tools, who can still be found in New Guinea, are more politic: they sympathize with the fate of their axes when, once broken or done with, they refuse to cut down any more trees. The axes are not abandoned in the jungle, but returned to the village, where they can enjoy a well-deserved retirement. Still, it is striking how the myths about baskets stress their softness and limited durability. For the Tacana, the body of the supernatural master of basket making is made from a basket of green leaves, which is to say, from a type of basket that can scarcely be used more than once.

Throughout much of the New World, baskets are considered, relative to other objects, to be particularly sensitive. They come from nature, and after receiving their status as cultural objects from a sometimes perfunctory artisinal labor, they return to nature. They are already quite flimsy, and their fragility is accentuated by the fact that, once damaged, they cannot be put to new use in some other form. Yet simply to throw them into the garbage remains an act heavy with signification. Though no longer used, they conserve something of their cultural dignity; they inspire a certain vague respect, for one hesitates to mistreat objects that were once intimately associated with those who used them. Concerning the flexible baskets that were carried on the back, and until recently used for gathering by the Kalapuya (an isolated linguistic group, south of the estuary of the Columbia River), an indigenous informant said, "It is something that the women constantly had with them."

Corpses are like baskets whose time is up; they are the remains that the soul or souls (or in the case of baskets, their spirits) are loathe to quit. In America, moreover, there is something equivalent, or almost equivalent, to internment for baskets: according to the Pomo, when a basket spirit dies, it remains in the ground for four days before ascending to the sky.

Japanese beliefs move in the opposite direction. Abandoned utensils may change into supernatural spirits, but it is advisable to burn old things, or at any rate, get rid of them. A traveler, who sought shelter in an abandoned temple, witnessed during the night the dance of an old winnowing basket, a cloth square (a *furoshiki,* used to transport packages), and an old drum: "This is what happens when you forget to throw out things that are used up." A frontier must be traced between yesterday and today, and between today and tomorrow, as with the Japanese lady who was held up to me as an example (though she is probably not exceptional), who did her laundry every day for fear that she might die suddenly and leave her dirty linen behind.

We are always confronted with the following choice: we can break with the past, including the recent past; or we can keep—though for how long?—our old clothes and the old things that have hollowed out a place for themselves in our existence and become like dear deceased friends. Let us end with Baudelaire:

> My boots! shall go back to that wardrobe's gloom
> Which shall encoffin you.*

---

*O mes bottes! rentrez au fond de cette armoire
Qui va vous servir de cercueil.

24

In the tribes of the North American Plains, the men painted figurative scenes or abstract designs on bison skins or other surfaces. The art of embroidering porcupine quills was reserved for
the women. The techniques involved in flattening, softening, and
dying the needles of different lengths and resistances and then in
folding, tying, weaving, interlacing, and sewing them were quite
difficult and required years of apprenticeship. The sharp quills
could cause injuries and even blindness, should they jump, like little springs, into the eyes.

Although purely decorative in appearance, quill work in geo-
metric patterns was laden with meaning. The quill worker meditated at length on the form and content of her work; alternatively,
she received her inspiration in a dream or vision revealed by a
two-faced divinity, the mother of the arts. Once a woman had
been inspired by the goddess with a design, her companions

would copy it and it became part of the tribal repertory. But the creator herself would be considered someone special.

According to an old Indian, speaking almost a century ago:

> When a woman dreams of the Double Woman, from that time on, in everything she makes, no one excels her. But then the woman is very much like a crazy woman. She laughs uncontrollably and so time and time again she acts deceptively. So the people are very afraid of her. She causes all men who stand near her to become possessed. For that reason these women are called Double Women. They are very promiscuous. . . . But then in the things they make nobody excels them. They do much quillwork. From then on, they are very skillful. They also work like a man.

This astonishing portrait of the artistic genius goes far beyond the imagery of the romantics, or the cliché, which appeared later in the century, of the accursed poet or painter, with all its pseudophilosophical elaborations concerning the relation between art and madness. Where we speak in a figurative sense, preliterate peoples express themselves literally. One has only to transpose the sense of the terms to see that they are not very different from us, or that we are not very different from them.

On Canada's Pacific coast, among the Tsimshian, painters and sculptors formed a special category, designated by a collective noun that evoked the mystery surrounding them. The man, woman, or even child who surprised them at their work was immediately put to death. Such cases have been corroborated. In these very hierarchical societies, the status of artist was hereditary among the nobles, but could be bequeathed to a commoner whose gifts had been recognized. The novice, whether noble or plebeian, underwent long and severe tests of initiation. The incumbent artist had to project his magical gifts onto the body of his successor. It was said that the latter, ravished by the protective spirit of the artist, disappeared into the heavens. Actually, he would remain hidden for a time in the forest, before reappearing in public, invested with his new powers.

The masks—both the simple and jointed masks—that the artists alone had the right and skill to construct were formidable entities. According to a well-read Indian at the turn of this century, a supernatural spirit called Boiling Words

> has a body like that of a dog. The chief did not wear it on his face or on his head, because the mask had its own body, and it was considered a very terrible object. Its whistle was very hard. Nobody now knows how to do it. It is not blown with the mouth, but it is squeezed on a certain mark on the whistle. All they know about this being was that it was living in a rock of the mountain. They had a song of his mask. It was always kept hidden, and no common people knew about it, only the children of the head chief and the children of the head man of Dzebasa's tribe. The children were very much afraid to hear the voice of Boiling Words. It was a very terror among the common people, and it was a great cause of pride among the princes and princesses to be allowed to touch it. It was very expensive to obtain the right to use it.

The artists had many other responsibilities: they decorated the façades of houses and, within the latter, the portable partitions; they sculpted the heraldic poles and house posts; and they constructed ritual instruments and parade objects. But above all, it was their responsibility to conceive, construct, and operate the machinery that gave the social and religious ceremonies of the region the appearance of spectacular stage shows. The latter were presented in the open air, or else in their dwelling places, which formed of a single vast room housing several families, could accommodate a large number of guests.

One indigenous story, dating from the last century, describes a performance during the course of which the hearth in the middle of the room was suddenly submerged by water rising from the depths—as at the end of *The Twilight of the Gods*. A full-size whalelike creature appeared, snorting and spurting water out of its blowholes. It then dived, after which the water disappeared, the soil became dry, and the fire was relit.

One did not tolerate any mistakes by the inventors and director–producers of these incredible mechanical devices. In 1895 Boas published the story of a ceremony whose highlight was to be the return of a man "from a visit to the bottom of the sea." The spectators massed on the beach saw a rock emerge from the water, open up, and a man step out. The stagehands, hidden in the woods, were operating the device from a distance with the help of ropes. They succeeded twice (the audience demanded encores), but on the third try the ropes became entangled, and the rock sank with the man in it. The man's family, hiding their grief, proclaimed that he had decided to remain at the ocean bottom, and the festive occasion continued as planned. But once the guests had departed, the deceased's family and those responsible for the disaster "tied themselves to a long rope . . . and precipitated themselves from a cliff into the sea."

Another story relates how, in order to stage an initiate's return to earth, the artists constructed a whale out of seal skins, which was activated by means of ropes. For greater realism, they had water inside that they brought to a boil by plunging red–hot stones into it, so as to make steam come out of the blowholes. A stone fell to the side and burned a hole in the skin, causing the whale to sink. The ceremony's organizers and the whale's creators all committed suicide, knowing that they would be put to death by the guardians of the mystery plays.

These stories come from the Tsimshian Indians, who live on the northern coast of British Columbia. The myths of their Haida neighbors on the Queen Charlotte Islands, just across the way, tell of villages located at the bottom of the seas or in the depths of the forests, which are inhabited by a people of artists. It is as a result of their encounters with this people that the Indians learned how to paint and sculpt. As such, these myths too attribute a supernatural origin to the fine arts.

Yet in the ceremonies—and I have just given a few examples—everything appears to be a matter of artifice: from the solemn performance in which the initiator claims (and presumably believes, but to what extent?) to be inhabited by a supernatural spirit that he draws out from his own body to discharge violently onto that of the novice cowering beneath a mat, as a whistle, the spirit's acoustic symbol, is blown; to the fabrication of the masks and mechanical devices in which the spirit's presence is said to be manifest; right up to the prodigious spectacles described by some of their last witnesses.

It is the aesthetic emotion produced by a successful spectacle that retroactively validates the belief in its supernatural origins. This is even the case, it has to be said, for the spectacle's creators and actors, though, because they are fully aware of the use of artifice, the ceremony's relation to the supernatural takes on, at best, a somewhat hypothetical character: "It must have been true because, despite all the difficulties which we busted our brains trying to come up with, it still succeeded." On the other hand, a failed spectacle, by revealing the underlying trickery, risks shattering the conviction that the human and supernatural worlds are intimately connected, a conviction of considerable import, given that, in these hierarchical societies, the power of the nobles, the subordination of the commoners, and the subjugation of the slaves, in short, the entire social order, were sanctioned by, and thus depended on, the supernatural order.

We do not condemn to death (or not to a physical death, perhaps an economic or social death) artists whom we deem devoid of talent because they do not take us beyond ourselves. But do we not still perceive a link between art and the supernatural? This is the etymological root of the word *enthusiasm,* which we use to convey what we experience before great works or art. Formerly one spoke of the "divine" Raphael, and in its aesthetic vocabulary, the English language contains the expression "out of this world." Here, too, one has only to convert the literal meaning of beliefs and practices that may offend or disconcert us into its figurative sense in order to perceive a certain similarity with our own beliefs and practices.

Among the Amerindians of this region, the condition of the artist has a disquieting, if not a sinister connotation. To be sure, artists are placed high up on the social scale, but they are dedicated to deceit and killed or forced to commit suicide should they fail. At the same time, the portrait of the artist presented by the myths of this region is full of poetry and charm.

The immediate neighbors of the Tsimshian, the Tlingit of Alaska, tell of a young chief of the Queen Charlotte Islands, in Haida territory, who loved his wife dearly. She fell sick and, in spite of all his efforts, died. The grief-stricken husband wandered from place to place in search of a carver who could reproduce a likeness of the deceased. Now, in his village, there lived a renowned carver, who, on meeting the widower one day, said:

> "You are going from village to village to have wood carved like your wife's face, and you can not find anyone to do it, can you? I have seen your wife a great deal walking along with you. I have never studied her face with the idea that you might want someone to carve it, but I am going to try if you will allow me."
>
> The carver got hold of a piece of red cedar and set to work. When his carving was finished, he dressed it in her clothes and called the husband. Overjoyed, the husband took the statue and asked the carver how much he owed him. "Do as you please

about it." The carver had felt sorry to see how this chief was mourning for his wife, so he said, "It is because I felt badly for you that I made that. So don't pay me too much for it." He paid the carver very well, however, both in slaves and in goods.

Here is an artist who is so famous that not even a notable dared seek him out; who believes that before undertaking a portrait, one should have studied the model's physiognomy; who does not allow anyone to watch him at work; who, on occasion, demonstrates his humanity and selflessness; and whose works are quite valuable. Isn't this the ideal portrait of a great painter or sculptor, even a contemporary one? Would that all our own artists were of a similar character.

The young chief, the myth goes on, treated the statue as though it were alive. One day, he even had the impression that it had moved. Visitors went into raptures over the resemblance. With time, the statue appeared to take on an increasingly human likeness (no doubt we can guess where this is going). But, in fact, a short time later, the statue gave forth a sound like that of cracking wood. The statue was lifted up, and a small tree that had been growing underneath it was discovered. The tree was allowed to grow very large, and that is why red cedars on the Queen Charlotte Islands are so beautiful. When after a search, one finds a good, strong tree, one says: "This looks like the baby of the chief's wife." As for the statue, it almost never moved, and no one ever heard it speak, but the husband knew by his dreams that she was addressing him and understood what she was saying.

The Tsimshian (whose art the Tlingit greatly admired and often ordered) tell the story differently. It is the widower himself who carves the statue of the deceased. He treats it as if it were alive and pretends to converse with it, making up questions and responses. One day two sisters enter his cabin, hide themselves, and see him kiss and hug the wooden statue. This makes them laugh, and they are discovered by the man, who invites them for dinner. The younger one eats with discretion, but the older sister overeats. Later, while sleeping, the elder one gets diarrhea and soils the bed. The younger sister and the widower decide to marry and make the following promise to each other: he will destroy the statue and keep quiet about her sister's shame, and she will not "tell anyone what [he had] done to the wooden figure."

The parallelism between the (quantitative) vice of gluttony and the (qualitative) vice of sexual incontinence is striking, for both suggest a perversion of communication. Moreover, to copulate with a statue as though it were human and to eat to excess appear, in their distinct registers, all the more comparable as many languages (including French, at a metaphorical level at least) often use akin words for "eating" and "copulating."

The Tlingit and Tsimshian myths, however, do not treat their common theme in the same manner. The second myth disapproves of the wooden figure's being mistaken for a human being. Admittedly, the statue was the work of a rank amateur, and I have spoken of the mystery with which, as highly prized professionals, the Tsimshian painters and sculptors surrounded their work. To have their art seen as lifelike was both their privilege and their obligation. As the purpose of the illusion created by a work of art was to attest to the ties binding the social to the supernatural order, one would have frowned upon any ordinary individual who used art's enchantment for his or her own particular, sentimental ends. In the eyes of public opinion, as represented by the two sisters, the conduct of the widower enamored of a simulacrum must have appeared scandalous or, at the very least, ridiculous.

The Tlingit myth provides a very different conception of the work of art. The widower's conduct does not shock; on the contrary, there is a crush of people trying to get into his house and admire the masterpiece. But the statue's creator was a famous master carver, and (despite or because of this fact) it remained as if suspended between art and life. Vegetal life begets only more vegetal life, and the woman in wood can give birth only to a tree. The Tlingit myth makes art into an autonomous realm, such that the work falls short of and goes beyond the intentions of the creator. Once the artist has created a work of art, he loses control of it, and it develops according to its own nature. In other words, the only way for a work of art to live on is to give rise to other artworks that will appear, to their contemporaries, more true to life than those that immediately preceded them.

Seen from the scale of millennia, the human passions blur. Time neither adds nor subtracts anything from the loves and hates experienced by the human species, nor from its commitments, struggles, and hopes: past and present always remain the same. Were some ten or twenty centuries of history to be suppressed at random, our understanding of human nature would not be appreciably affected. The only irreplaceable loss would be that of the works of art created during this period. For men and women differ, and even exist, only through their works. Like the wooden statue that gave birth to a tree, they alone bear evidence that, among human beings, something actually happened during the course of time.

Works Cited

1

Proust, M., *A l'ombre des jeunes filles en fleurs*, deuxième partie: "noms de pays: le pays"; *Remembrance of Things Past*. Vol. III, New York, Random House, 1981, pp. 882, 937, 1090. Curtis, J.-L., *Lectures en liberté*, Paris, Flammarion, 1991, p. 86.

2

Schapiro, M., "Seurat and *La Grande Jatte*," *Columbia Review*, 1935. Diderot, D., "Essais sur la peinture," in *Oeuvres esthétiques*, Paris, Garnier, 1959, pp. 719, 825. Champaigne, Ph. de, cited by J. Thuillier, "Pour un Corpus pussinianum," in *Actes du Colloque international Nicolas Poussin*, Paris, [publisher unknown] 1960, p. 159. Delacroix, E., *Journal*, Sept. 23, 1854, April 27, 1853, April 28, 1853, June 16, 1851, Nov. 1, 1852, June 6, 1851, May 11, 1847, Feb. 27, 1850, New York, Grove Press, 1961. Coypel, A., "L'esthétique du peintre," in *Conférences de l'Académie royale de peinture et de sculpture*, published by H. Join, Paris, Quantin, 1883, p. 315. Ingres,

J. D., "Notes et pensées," in H. Delaborde, *Ingres, sa vie, ses travaux, sa doctrine d'après les notes manuscrites et les lettres du maître*, Paris, Plon, 1870, p. 136 [I have consulted Walter Pach, *Ingres*, New York, Harper and Bros., 1939]. Félibien, A., *Journal*, cited by J. Thuillier, op. cit., p. 80; *Entretiens sur la vie et les ouvrages des plus excellens peintres anciens et modernes*, Nouvelle édition revue et corrigée, Trévoux, imprimerie du S.A.S. 6 volumes, 1725, vol. IV, *Huitième Entretien;* "Vie de Poussin," in *Lettres de Nicolas Poussin*, etc., Paris, Wittmann, 1945, pp. 13–14. Blunt, A., *Nicolas Poussin, I, Text; II, Plates* (A.W. Mellon Lectures in the Fine Arts), Washington D.C., 1967, I, pp. 242–44.

3

Panofsky, E., "*Et in Arcadia ego*: On the Conception of Transience in Poussin and Watteau," in *Philosophy and History: Essays Presented to Ernst Cassirer*, Oxford, Clarendon Press, 1936; republished in *Meaning in the Visual Arts*, Garden City, N.Y., Doubleday Anchor Books, 1955. Diderot, D., *Oeuvres complètes*, publ. by J. Assézat, Paris, 1875–1877. Jaucourt, chevalier de, art. "Paysagiste" in *Encyclopédie*.

4

Félibien, A., *Entretiens, op. cit.*, pp. 90–115. Champaigne, Ph. de, in *Conférences de l'Académie*, etc., op. cit., p. 91. Reynolds, Sir J., *Seven Discourses Delivered in the Royal Academy by the President*, San Marino, Calif., Huntington, 1959, p. 158. Le Brun, Ch., cited by A. Fontaine, *Les Doctrines d'art en France: Peintres, amateurs, critiques de Poussin à Diderot*, Paris, Laurens, 1909, p. 82. Piles, R. de, *Conversa-*

tions sur la connoissance de la peinture, etc., A Paris chez Nicolas Lan-
glis, 1677, p. 260.

5

Conférences de l'Académie, etc., op. cit., pp. 90–97. Yoe, M. R.,
"Catlin's Indians," *Johns Hopkins Magazine,* June 1983, p. 29.
Diderot, D., *Salon de 1763* (see under 11). Goncourt, E. & J. de,
"Chardin," *Gazette des Beaux-Arts,* 163–64. Pascal, Bl., *Pensées,* II,
Paris, Lemerre, 1879, p. 150. Seznec, J., "John Martin en France,"
All Souls Studies IV, London, Faber & Faber, 1964, pp. 48–49. Plu-
tarque, "Propos de Table," in *Les Oeuvres meslées,* trans. by Amyot,
Paris, 1584, II, p. 119. Chabanon, M.P.G. de, *De la Musique* (see un-
der 14), p. 50. Rousseau, J.-J., *Lettre sur la musique française.* Morellet,
Abbé A., *Mélanges de littérature et de philosophie,* 4 vol., Paris 1818, IV,
p. 395.

6

Ingres, J.A.D., "Notes et pensées," *op. cit.,* pp. 115, 129, 132, 133,
136, 150, 153, 159, 162. Delacroix, E., *Journal,* Jan. 13, 1857, Oct. 17,
1853. Félibien, A., *Entretiens, op. cit.,* III, p. 194; IV, pp. 13, 113,
155–56. Diderot, D., "Essais sur la peinture," *op. cit.,* 834. Blanc,
Ch., *Les Artistes de mon temps,* Paris, Firmin Didot, 1876, pp. 23–24,
72. Delacroix, E., cited in E. Amaury-Duval, *L'Atelier d'Ingres,* publ.
by Élie Faure, 3d ed., Paris, Crès, 1924, pp. 12, 241. Baudelaire, C.,
Art in Paris: Salons and Other Exhibitions, trans. and ed. by Jonathan
Mayne, London, Phaidon Press, 1965. Menpes, M., "A Lesson from
Khiosi," *The Magazine of Art,* April 1888. Riegl, A., *Grammaire his-
torique des arts plastiques,* Paris, Klincksieck, 1978, p. 109.

7

Balzac, H. de, *Beatrix*. Chabanon, M.P.G. de, *De la Musique* (see under 14), p. 369. Wagner, R., *Lettres de . . . à ses amis*, trad. G. Khnopff, Paris, Félix Juven, s.s., no. LV (to Th. Uhlig). Amaury-Duval, E., *L'Atelier d'Ingres,* op. cit., p. 47. Wagner, Cosima, *Diaries,* vol. 2, London, Collins, 1980, p. 925. Wind, E., *Art and Anarchy,* New York, Alfred A. Knopf, 1964, p. 9. Newton, I. *Traité d'Optique,* etc., trad. Coste, 2d French ed., Paris, Montalant, 1722, pp. 241, 335–36, 449, 513.

8

Adam, A., "Rameau," *Revue contemporaine,* Oct. 15, 1852; *Derniers Souvenirs d'un musicien,* Paris, Michel Lévy frères, 1859, pp. 61–62. Masson, P.-M., *L'Opéra de Rameau,* Paris, Henri Laurens, 1930, p. 491. [Anonymous], *Réponse à la critique de l'opéra de Castor et observations sur la musique,* Paris, 1773, pp. 38–39, 43–44, 45. Rameau, J. Ph., *Oeuvres complètes,* published under the direction of C. Saint-Saëns, Paris, Durand, vol. VIII, 1903. Lajarte, Th. de, *Castor et Pollux,* score for piano and voice, Paris, Th. Michelis, s.d., p. 3. Rameau, J.-Ph., *Castor et Pollux,* Bibliothèque nationale, Vm 2 331 & 334.

9

Adam, A., *Derniers Souvenirs,* etc., *op. cit.,* p. 61. [Anonymous], *Mercure de France,* July 1782, pp. 42–43, 45. [Chabanon], "Sur la Musique, à l'occasion de *Castor,*" *Mercure de France,* April 1772, pp. 165–66. Chabanon, M.P.G. de, *Éloge de M. Rameau,* Paris, Lambert,

1764, p. 36; *De la musique*, etc. (see under 14), pp. 116, 192. Rameau, J.-Ph., *Code de musique pratique*, etc., Paris, Imprimerie Royale, 1760, p. 168. Berlioz, H., "De Rameau et de quelques-uns de ses ouvrages," *Revue et gazette musicale*, 1842, p. 442. Masson, P.-M., *L'Opéra de Rameau,* op. cit., pp. 218, 255, 443, 480–81.

––––––––

10

Diderot, D., "Essais sur la peinture," in *Oeuvres esthétiques*, Paris, Garnier, 1959, pp. 718, 765. Wind, E., *Pagan Mysteries in the Renaissance*, Harmondsworth, Penguin Books, 1967, pp. 113–27. Rousseau, J.-J., *Essai sur l'origine des langues*, ch. XIII, XVI. Starobinski, J., "Présentation," in *ibid.*, coll. Folio, Paris, Gallimard, 1990, p. 43. Batteux, Abbé Ch., *Les Beaux-Arts réduits à un même principe*, Paris, Chez Durand, 1746, pp. 260, 263, 269. Rousseau, J.-J., "De l'Imitation théatrale. Essai tiré des dialogues de Platon," in *Oeuvres complètes*, Paris, Desiez, 1837, II, pp. 183–91. Ingres, J. A. D., "Notes et pensées," *op. cit.*, p. 123.

––––––––

11

Poussin, N., "Lettre à Jacques Stella" in Félibien, *Entretiens, loc. cit.* Le Brun, Ch., "Discours sur *La Manne,*" in *Conférences de l'Académie*, etc., *op. cit.*, pp. 61–62. Félibien, A., *Entretiens, loc. cit.*, pp. 139–41. Diderot, D., art. "Composition" in *Encyclopédie*; *Salons*, Text established and presented by J. Seznec & J. Adhémar, 4 vol., Oxford, Clarendon Press, 1957–1967: Salons of 1759, 1763, 1767; "An Eulogy of Richardson" in *Diderot's Thoughts on Art and Style,* trans. and ed. by Beatrix Tollemache, New York, Burt Franklin, 1971, pp. 268–69.

WORKS CITED

12

Diderot, D., art. "Beau" in *Encyclopédie*; *Lettre sur les sourds et muets*, edition presented by P.-H. Meyer *(Diderot Studies VII)*, Geneva, Droz, 1965, pp. 70–89, 101, 163, 212. Gilman, M., *Imagination and Creation in Diderot (Diderot Studies II)*, Geneva, Droz, 1952, p. 214. Batteux, Ch., *Les Beaux-Arts*, etc., *op. cit.*, pp. 94, 169–73. Poussin, N., *Lettres et propos sur l'art*, Texts assembled and presented by Anthony Blunt, 2nd ed., Paris, Hermann, 1989, p. 45.

13

Kant, E., *Critique of Judgement*, Book II. Mandelbrot, B., *Fractals: Form, Chance and Dimension*, San Francisco, W. H. Freeman & Co., 1977. Duval, P. M., *Les Celtes* (L'Univers des Formes), Paris, Gallimard, 1977. Balzac, H. de, *Gambara*. Rosen, Ch., *The Classical Style,* New York, Norton, 1972, pp. 413, 448. Dewdney, A. K., "Wallpaper for the Mind," *Scientific American*, September 1986, pp. 14–23.

14

Jakobson, R., *Language in Literature*, Cambridge, Mass., The Belknap Press of Harvard University Press, 1987, p. 457. Rousseau, J.-J., *Dictionnaire de musique*, art. "Harmonie"; *Essay on the Origin of Languages*, ch. XIV. Batteux, Ch., *Les Beaux-Arts*, etc., op. cit., p. 281. Helmoltz, H. von, *Théorie physiologique de la musique*, Paris, Gabay, 1990, p. 406. Tamba, A., "Le concept japonais de création," *Traverses*, nos. 38–39, November 1986, p. 232. Lord, A.B., *The Singer of Tales*, Cambridge, Mass., Harvard University Press, 1960, p. 30. Michotte,

E., *Richard Wagner's Visit to Rossini and An Evening at Rossini's in Beau-Sejour*, University of Chicago Press, 1968 (1860), p. 60. Chabanon, M.P.G. de, *De la Musique considérée en elle-même et dans ses rapports avec la parole, les langues, la poésie et le théâtre*, Paris, Pissot, 1785, pp. 50–53, 56–60, 158, 355. Morellet, A., "De l'Expression en musique," *Mercure de France*, November 1771, p. 123. Chabanon, M.P.G. de, *Éloge de M. Rameau*, op. cit., p. 16.

15

Chabanon, M.P.G. de, *De la Musique*, etc., op. cit., pp. 27, 29, 30–33, 38, 49, 65, 73, 115–16, 135, 166, 168, 169, 171, 193, 201–2, 207–9, 213–14, 348, 400, 407, 442–43; *Éloge,* op. cit., pp. 22–23, 38, 45–48. Rousseau, J.-J., *Lettre sur la musique française*. Sherlock, M., *Nouvelles Lettres d'un voyageur anglais*, London and Paris, 1780, pp. 161–207. Batteux, Ch., "Traité de la construction oratoire" in *Principes de la Littérature*, Paris, 1774, vol. V, 2nd part, ch. I and II.

16

Chabanon, M.P.G. de, *De la Musique*, etc., *op. cit.*, pp. 3, 73, 84, 133, 371, 393, 447–50, 456, 459. Rousseau, J.-J., art. "Musique" in *Encyclopédie*. Lévi-Strauss, C., *The Raw and the Cooked*, New York, Harper and Row, 1970, p. 19. Marmontel, J.-F., art. "Arts libéraux" in *Supplément à l'Encyclopédie*, vol. I, Amsterdam, Rey, 1776; *Mémoires d'un père pour servir à l'instruction de ses enfans*, 4 vol., in *Ouevres posthumes*, Paris 1804. Chabanon, M.P.G. de, *Observations sur la musique et principalement sur la métaphysique de l'art*, Paris, 1779.

17

Chabanon, M.P.G. de, *Éloge, op. cit.*, pp. 32, 34, 54; *De la Musique*, etc., *op. cit.*, pp. 2–3, 92–93, 95–96, 98–99, 101, 184, 235–37, 291, 293, 296, 298, 302, 359.

18

Leiris, M., *Operratiques*, Paris, P.O.L., 1992, pp. 47, 51, 57, 105–6, 110, 117–19, 131, 135, 190; *Journal 1922–1989*, Paris, Gallimard, 1992, pp. 485–87. Lévi-Strauss, C., *The Raw and the Cooked, op. cit.*, pp. 14–18; "From Chrétien de Troyes to Richard Wagner," in *The View from Afar*, New York, Basic Books, 1985, Chapter 17. Chabanon, M.P.G. de, *De la Musique*, etc., *op. cit.*, pp. 36, 46, 192, 261, 263, 266, 268–69, 270–72, 277, 283, 287, 304, 305, 308–13, 334n., 363; *Éloge*, op. cit., p. 22. La Bruyère, J. de, *Les Caractères*, ch. I. Batteux, Ch., *Les Beaux-Arts*, etc., *op. cit.*, p. 211. Wagner, R., *Lettres de . . . à ses amis*, op. cit., XXIV, XXV (to F. Heine). Hannetaire, D', *Réflexions sur l'Art du comédien*, 4th ed., 1776, p. 27. Lévi-Strauss, C., *The Naked Man*, New York, Harper and Row, 1981, pp. 646–47, 652–53.

19

Castel, R. B., *L'Optique des couleurs*, Paris, chez Briasson, 1740, pp. 46–57, 105, 118, 156–58, 210–11, 302, 305, 314, 431, 446; *Description de l'orgue ou du clavecin oculaire* [. . .] *par le célèbre M. Tellemann, Musicien, ibid.*, pp. 473–87. Parra, F., "Les bases physiologiques de la vision des couleurs," in S. Tornay, ed., *Voir et nommer les couleurs,*

Nanterre, Laboratoire d'ethnologie et de sociologie comparative, 1978. Albright, Th. D., "Color and the integration of motion signals," *Trends in Neuroscience*, vol. 14, no. 7, 1991. Rimbaud, A., *Complete Works, Selected Letters*, Trans., Intro., and Notes by W. Fowlie, Chicago, University of Chicago Press, 1966. Jakobson, R. (with Linda Waugh), *The Sound Shape of Language*, Bloomington, Indiana University Press, 1979, p. 193. Clavière, J., "L'audition colorée," *Année Psychologique* 5, 1899, pp. 171–72, Valéry, P., "Triomphe de Manet" in *Manet*, Paris, Orangerie, 1932: XIV–XVI. Rimbaud, A., *Complete Works*, op. cit.: *Being Beauteous, Les Mains de Marie-Jeanne, Les Premières Communions, Mes Petites Amoureuses, Michel et Christine*. Baudelaire, Ch., *Oeuvres complètes*, Pléiade, 1961: *Salon de 1846, L'Idéal, Le Possédé, Harmonie du Soir*. Jakobson, R. (with J. Lotz), "Notes on the French Phonemic Pattern," in *Selected Writings*, vol. I, 'S-Gravenhage, Mouton, 1962, p. 431; *The Sound Shape*, etc., op. cit., pp. 151–52. Gautier, Th., "Haschich," *La Presse*, 10 juillet 1843. Mac Laury, R. E., "From Brightness to Hue: An Explanatory Model of Color-Category Evolution," *Current Anthropology*, vol. 33, no. 2, April 1992. Rimbaud, A., *Complete Works*, op. cit.: *Ce qu'on dit au poète, Denriers vers, L'Éclatante Victoire de Sarrebrück, Mes Petites Amoureuses, l'Orgie parisienne, Le Bateau Ivre*. Castel, R. B., *L'Optique des couleurs*, op. cit., pp. 135, 270, 400. Albright, Th. D., "Color and the Integration," etc., op. cit., p. 267n. Chabanon, M.P.G. de, *De la Musique*, etc., op. cit., p. 215. Jakobson, R., *The Sound Shape*, etc., op. cit., p. 133.

20

Lévi-Strauss, C., *Tristes Tropiques*, New York, Atheneum, 1963, p. 26.

21

Lévi-Strauss, C., *The Naked Man, op. cit.*, pp. 694–95. Gobineau, A. de., *Selected Political Writings*, Edited and Introduced by Michael D. Biddiss, London, Jonathan Cape, 1970, p. 176.

22

Boas, F., "Decorative Designs of Alaskan Needle-cases," etc., *Proceedings of the U.S. National Museum*, vol. 34, 1908; republished in *Race, Language and Culture*, New York, Macmillan, 1940, pp. 588–89. Demetracopoulou, Lee D., cited by C. Lévi-Strauss, *Structural Anthropology*, New York, Basic Books, 1963, p. 174. Walker, J. R., "The Sun Dance and other Ceremonies of the Oglala Division of the Teton Dakota," *Anthropological Papers of the American Museum of Natural History*, vol. XVI, part II, 1917, pp. 194–95. Kant, E., *Critique of Judgement*, First Part, Second Book, §53. Ingres, J. A. D., "Notes et pensées," op. cit., pp. 95–96. Boas, F., *Primitive Art*, Oslo, H. Aschenhoug and Co., 1927, pp. 29, 46–54, and *passim*. Benvensite, E., *Problems in General Linguistics,* Coral Gables, University of Miami Press, 1971, pp. 281–88. Cabanne, P., *Entretiens avec Marcel Duchamp*, Paris, Belfond, 1967, pp. 57–58.

23

Diderot-D'Alembert, *Encylopédie*: art. "Vannerie," "Mandrerie," "Closerie," "Faisserie," "Lasserie," *La Grande Encyclopédie*, Paris, 1885–1903: art. "Vannerie." Shackelford, R. S., "Legend of the Klickitat Basket," *American Anthropologist*, II, 1900, pp. 779–80. Holmes, W. M., "A Study of the Textile Art, etc.," *Sixth Annual Re-*

port, Bureau of American Ethnology (1884–1885), Washington, D.C., 1888, fig. 289, p. 199. Barrett, S. A., *Pomo Myths*, Milwaukee *(Bulletin of the Public Museum,* vol. 15), 1933, pp. 124, 301–2, 380–82. Hill-Tout, Ch., *The Natives of British North America*, London, 1907, p. 113. Eells, M., *The Indians of Puget Sound. The Notebook of. . .* , Seattle, University of Washington Press, 1985, p. 96. Haeberlin, H. K., & E. Gunther, "The Indians of Puget Sound," *University of Washington Publications in Anthropology*, 4/1, 1930, p. 33. Jacobs, M., "Kalapuya Texts," *ibid.*, 11, 1945, pp. 20, 25, 37–38. Haeberlin, H. K., J. A. Teit, & H. H. Roberts, "Coiled Basketry in British Columbia," *Forty-first Annual Report, Bureau of American Ethnology* (1919–1924), Washington, D.C., 1928, p. 390. Sapir, E., "Wishram Texts," *Publications of the American Ethnological Society*, 2, Leyden, 1909, p. 35. Adamson, Th., "Folk-Tales of the Coast Salish," *Memoirs of the American Folk-Lore Society*, XVII, New York, 1934, p. 254. Ballard, A .C., "Mythology of Southern Puget Sound," *University of Washington Publications in Anthropology*, 3/2, 1929, p. 104. Boas, F., "Zur Mythologie der Indianer von Washington und Oregon," *Globus*, 63, 1893. Jacobs, M., "Northwest Sahaptin Texts," *Columbia University Contributions to Anthropology*, 19/1–2, 1834, pp. 188–89. Cadogan, L., "Ayvu Rapita, etc.," *Antropologia* 5, *Boletim* 227, Universidade de Sao Paulo, 1959, p. 82. Clastres, P., *Le Grand Parler*, Paris, Seuil, 1974, pp. 76–77. Magalhaes, Couto de, *O Selvagem*, 4th ed., Sao Paulo, Biblioteca Pedagogica Brasileira, 1940, p. 233. Hissink, K. & A. Hahn, *Die Tacana. I. Erzählungsgut*, Stuttgart, Kohlhammer Verlag, 1961, pp. 85, 226, 367. Toth, N., D. Clark & G. Ligabue, "The Last Stone Axe Makers," *Scientific American*, July 1992, pp. 67–71. Ikeda, H., *A Type and Motif Index of Japanese Folk Literature (FF Communications,* vol. XCIX, no. 209), Helsinki, Academia Scientiarum Fennica, 1971, p. 326 (B, C, G). Yanagita, K., *Japanese Folk Tales*, Tokyo New Service, 1966, pp. 60–61. Baudelaire, Ch., "Mes Bottes. Élégie refusée aux jeux floraux," *Oeuvres complètes*, op. cit., p. 268–69.

WORKS CITED

24

Walker, J. R., *Lakota Belief and Ritual*, Lincoln, University of Nebraska Press, 1991, pp. 165–66. Boas, F., "Tsimshian Mythology," *Thirty-first Annual Report, Bureau of American Ethnology* (1909–1910), Washington, D.C., 1916, pp. 152–54, 555. Seguin, M. (ed.), *The Tsimshian. Images of the Past. Views from the Present*, Vancouver, University of British Columbia Press, 1984, pp. 164, 287–88. Boas, F., "The Nass River Indians," in *Report of the British Association for the Advancement of Science for 1895*, London, p. 580. Swanton, J. R., "Haida Texts," *Memoirs of the American Museum of Natural History*, vol. XIV, New York, 1908, pp. 457, 489. "Tlingit Myths and Texts," *Bulletin 39, Bureau of American Ethnology*, Washington, D.C., 1909, pp. 181–82.

Index

*Abduction from the Seraglio,
The* (Mozart), 124
Adam, Adolphe, 42, 47,
48, 50, 51–52
Alembert, Jean Le Rond
d', 43, 46
Alembert's Dream, D'
(Diderot), 95
Amaury-Duval, Eugène,
36, 45
Amerindians, 182
Amyot, Jacques, 105
Apollinaire, Gauillaume,
147, 151
Apollo and Daphne (Rim-
baud), 11
Aragon, Louis, 150
Armide (Gluck), 55, 122

Bach, Johann Sebastian,
56
Bacon, Francis, 80
Balzac, Honoré de, 43,
44, 86
Balzac, Jean-Louis Guez
de, 105
Barbieri, Giovanni
Francesco. *See* Guer-
cino, Il
Basket making, 169–76
Bathers of Valpinçon, The
(Ingres), 33
Batteux, Charles, abbé,

68, 78, 79, 92, 100,
105, 122
Baudelaire, Charles, 36,
95, 134, 176
"Beauty, On" (Diderot),
77–78, 81
*Beaux-Arts réduits à un
même principe, Les* (Bat-
teux), 68
Beethoven, Ludwig van,
43, 44–45, 86, 99
Bellori, Giovanni Pietro,
18
Benveniste, Emile, 165
Berlioz, Hector, 54, 55
Berthelot, André, 47
Bizet, Georges, 117
Blanc, Charles, 34
*Blind Orion Searching for
the Rising Sun* (Rim-
baud), 11
Blunt, Anthony, 13
Boas, Franz, 159–60, 161,
164–65, 180
Boron, Robert de, 116
Botticelli, Sandro, 66
Bourdon, Sébastien, 19
Braque, Georges, 147
Breton, André, 143–51
Breton, Elisa, 143
*Bride Stripped Bare by her
Bachelors, The*
(Duchamp), 27–28

Cadogan, Leon, 173
Caillois, Roger, 148
Caliari, Paul. *See*
Veronese, Paul
Caravaggio, 34
Carmen (Bizet), 117
Castel, P. Louis-Bertrand,
129–32, 137–38, 140
Castor et Pollux (Rameau),
41–42, 47–57, 99
Catlin, George, 27
Chabanon, Michel-Paul-
Guy de, 28, 43–44, 53,
55, 93–94, 95, 97–114,
117–18, 119–20, 121,
122–24, 139
Champaigne, Philippe
de, 10, 19, 20, 22, 25,
26
Champmêlé, Marie, 119
Chapuis, Auguste, 49
Chardin, Jean-Baptiste
Siméon, 27, 28, 30,
75, 81
Chehalis, 172
Chinook, 172
Chrétien de Troyes, 117
Cimarosa, Domenico, 14,
43
Clastres, Pierre, 173
Clavière, Jean, 132
Clément, Félix, 42, 47
Colbert, Jean-Baptiste, 19

INDEX

Conferences on Painting and Sculpture (Royal Academy of Painting), 19, 25

Considérations sur les langues (Chabanon), 104

Conversation between D'Alembert and Diderot (Diderot), 131

Corneille, Pierre, 122

Corot, Jean-Baptiste Camille, 31

Così fan tutte (Mozart), 124

Coypel, Antoine, 12

Curtis, Jean-Louis, 5–6

Dali, Salvador, 147, 151

Death of Germanicus, The (Poussin), 72

Debussy, Claude, 43, 93, 94–95, 115

Delacroix, Eugène, 9, 10, 11–12, 13–14, 32, 34, 36, 84–86, 164

De la musique (Chabanon), 102, 113–14

Delille, Jacques, abbé, 18

Diderot, Denis, 9, 10, 18, 19, 27, 32, 47–48, 63–82, 95, 104, 117, 129, 131, 164

Donizetti, Gaetano, 117

Dubos, Jean-Baptiste, abbé, 18

Ducasse, Isidore. *See* Lautréamont, le comte de

Duchamp, Marcel, 27–28, 167

Duncan, Isadora, 99

Elements de Musique (Alembert), 43

Eliezer et Rebecca (Poussin), 19–23, 25–26

Elizabeth II, Queen of England, 130

Elléouët, Aube, 143

Éloge de M. Rameau (Chabanon), 102, 109–13

Enfant et les sortilèges, L' (Ravel), 124–25

Eribon, Didier, 50

Essay on the Inequality of the Human Races (Gobineau), 153–54

Essay on the Origin of Languages (Rousseau), 67–68, 104

Et in Arcadia ego (Guercino), 15–18

Et in Arcadia ego (Poussin), 15–19

Eyck, Jan van, 37

Farncombe, Charles, 50

Fauré, Gabriel, 5

Félibien, André, 13, 18, 19, 20, 33, 35, 37, 73

Flaxman, John, 36

Flying Dutchman, The (Wagner), 93

Fractals, 83–87

Franck, Cesar, 5

Gathering of the Manna (Poussin), 71, 73, 80

Gautier, Théophile, 135

Giotto di Bondone, 26–27

Gluck, Christoph-Willibald von, 53, 55, 93, 101, 122

Gobineau, Joseph-Arthur de, Comte, 153–54

Goncourt, Edmond and Jules de, 27

Grétry, André-Modeste, 165

Greuze, Jean-Baptiste, 74–75, 76, 81

Guarani, 173

Guayaki, 173–74

Guercino, Il, 15–18

Guimet, Emile, 36

Hannetaire, D', 119

Harnoncourt, Nicolaus, 49

Heure espagnole, L' (Ravel), 124

Hoffman, Ernst Theodor, 121

Hokusai Katsushika, 10

Homer, 161

Horace (Corneille), 122

Human Comedy, The (Balzac), 44

Hundred Views of Mount Fuji (Hokusai), 10

Illuminations (Rimbaud), 133–34

Ingres, Jean Auguste Dominique, 12, 32, 33, 34–35, 36–37, 45, 70, 163–64

Inuit, 159

Jakobson, Roman, 91, 132, 133, 135, 139

Japanese prints, 35–36, 37

Jaucourt, Louis Chevalier de, 18

Jolas, Betsy, 106

Journal (Leiris), 116

Judgment of Solomon, The (Poussin), 72

Jupiter and Thetis, The (Ingres), 33

Kalapuya, 175
Kant, Immanuel, 80, 83, 161
Kyôsai, Kawanabe, 36, 37

La Bruyère, Jean de, 120, 122
Lajarte, Théodore de, 50
Landscape with Polyphemus (Poussin), 32
Landscape with Pyramis and Thisbe (Poussin), 72
Laocoön, 19
Large Glass, The (Duchamp), 27–28
Larousse, Pierre, 41–42, 134–35
Lautréamont, le comte de, 147
Le Brun, Charles, 20, 21, 25, 73
Leibowitz, René, 115
Leiris, Michel, 115–17, 119, 121–22
Leoncavallo, Ruggero, 116
Le Sueur, Eustache, 14
Lesure, François, 50
Letter on the Deaf and Dumb (Diderot), 78, 79
Lohengrin (Wagner), 118
Lucia di Lammermoor (Donizetti), 117
Lully, Jean-Baptiste, 101, 121, 122

Magical Flute, The (Mozart), 124
Mahogany (Weill), 121
Malherbe, François de, 105
Mandelbrot, Benoit, 84
Manet, Edouard, 5, 133

Manfred Overture (Schumann), 45
Manifesto of Surrealism (Breton), 144
Mantegna, Andrea, 10–11
Marin (French officer), 106
Marmontel, Jean-François, 107–8
Martin, John, 28
Masson, Paul-Marie, 48, 49, 54, 55, 56
Maya, 174–75
Meistersinger, Der (Wagner), 116, 117
Mémoires (Marmontel), 108
Menotti, Gian Carlo, 115
Menpes, Mortimer, 36
Merisi, Michelangelo. See Caravaggio
Mer, La (Debussy), 93
Metastasio, Pietro, 122
Milhaud, Darius, 167
Monet, Claude, 5
Montaigne, Michel de, 105
Monteverdi, Claudio, 115
Morellet, André, abbé, 30, 93, 94, 108
Moses Striking Water from the Rock (Poussin), 73
Mozart, Wolfgang Amadeus, 14, 43, 45, 124

Naked Man, The (Lévi-Strauss), 121, 153
Nambikwara, 106
Neptune's Triumph (Ingres), 34
Newton, Isaac, 46n, 130
Ninth Symphony (Beethoven), 45, 99

Nude Descending a Staircase (Duchamp), 167
Nun, The (Diderot), 47–48

Octet for Wood Instruments (Stravinsky), 56
Odalisque and the Slave, The (Ingres), 33
Offenbach, Jacques, 124
Operratiques (Leris), 115–16
Opstal, Gérard Van, 19
Optics (Newton), 46n
Orion (Poussin), 32

Pagliacci (Leoncavallo), 116
Panofsky, Erwin, 16, 18, 66
Parnassus (Mantegna), 11
Parsifal (Wagner), 115, 116–17, 120
Pascal, Blaise, 27
Patinir, Joachim, 5
Pelléas et Mélisande (Debussy), 94–95, 115
Pergolèse, Jean-Baptiste, 53
Phèdre (Racine), 122
Picasso, Pablo, 147
Piles, Roger de, 22
Plains Indians, 27, 170, 177–78
Plato, 165
Plutarch, 28
Pomo, 170–71, 172, 174
Popol Vuh, 175
Poussin, Nicolas, 9–37, 71–73, 80, 164
Proust, Marcel, 5–7, 10
Puccini, Giacomo, 115–16

Quinault, Philippe, 121
Quittard, Henri, 47

INDEX

Racine, Jean, 119, 122
Rameau, Jean-Philippe, 39–57, 77, 92, 98, 99, 100, 101–2, 112, 119
Raphael, 182
Ravel, Maurice, 43, 124–25
Raw and the Cooked, The (Lévi-Strauss), 107
Régamey, Felix, 36
Rembrandt, 27
Remembrance of Things Past (Proust), 6
Reneville, Rolland de, 149–50
Reynolds, Joshua, 20
Richardson, Samuel, 75, 76
Ride of the Valkyries (Wagner), 118
Riegl, Aloïs, 37
Rimbaud, Arthur, 11, 132–41, 151
Ring cycle (Wagner), 117, 118
Roger Frees Angelica (Ingres), 33
Ronsard, Pierre de, 105
Rosen, Charles, 86
Rosenkavalier, Der (Strauss-Hofmannsthal), 94
Rossini, Gioacchino, 93, 124
Rouget, Gilbert, 50
Rousseau, Jean-Jacques, 28, 43, 46, 67–70, 91–92, 98, 99, 100, 101, 104, 105, 106, 129
Roussel, Raymond, 147, 151
Royal Academy of Painting, 19, 25
Rubens, Peter Paul, 34

Sachs, Hans, 116
Sahaptin, 172, 173
Saint-Saëns, Camille, 5, 49
Salish, 171, 172
Salons (Diderot), 19, 74, 76, 79–80, 81
Sanzio, Raffaello. *See* Raphael
Saussure, Ferdinand de, 91, 97, 102
Schapiro, Meyer, 9
Schubert, Franz, 5
Schumann, Robert, 45
Season in Hell, A (Rimbaud), 139, 149
Servandoni, Jean Nicolas. *See* Hannetaire, D'
Seurat, Georges, 9–10, 68
Sherlock, Martin, 99
Sioux, 160–61
Smith, Hélène, 151
Starobinski, Jean, 67
Stendhal, 134
Stratonice (Ingres), 33
Stravinsky, Igor, 43, 56
Sunday Afternoon on La Grande Jatte, A (Seurat), 9–10
Surrealist Situation of the Object (Breton), 144
Symphony in A (Mozart), 45

Tacana, 174, 175
Tannhäuser (Wagner), 118–19
Telemann, Georg Philipp, 129
Thompson Indians, 164
Thuillier, Jacques, 16
Time Regained (Proust), 6–7

Tlingit, 182–83, 184–85
Tosca (Puccini), 115–16
Tristan und Isolde (Wagner), 45
Trompe l'oeil, 27–30
Tsimshian, 178–81, 183–84
Tupi, 173–74
Tupi-Kawahib, 106
Turkish Bath, The (Ingres), 33, 34
Twilight of the Gods, The (Wagner), 180

Valéry, Paul, 133, 151
Van Dyck, Anthony, Sir, 34
Venus Presenting Arms to Aeneas (Rimbaud), 11
Vernet, Claude-Joseph, 75–76
Veronese, Paul, 34
Vien, Joseph Marie, 36
Village Bridge, The (Greuze), 74–75
Voltaire, 44, 121, 129
Vowels (Rimbaud), 132–41

Wagner, Cosima, 45
Wagner, Richard, 5, 44–45, 93, 115, 116–17, 118–19, 120, 121, 166, 180
Weill, Kurt, 121
Weyden, Rogier Van der, 37
Wind, Edgar, 45, 66
Wintu, 160

Zeami, 119